Gay Affirmative Ethics

Essays by
J. Michael Clark
Jeffrey Hopkins
Yoel H. Kahn
Bob McNeir
Craig W. Pilant
Michael L. Stemmeler

with a response by
Mark R. Kowalewski

Edited by
Michael L. Stemmeler
& J. Michael Clark

HQ
76.25
.G376
1993

Published by
Monument Press
Las Colinas, Texas

Copyright 1993, Monument Press

Library of Congress Cataloging-in-Publication Data

Gay affirmative ethics : essays / by J. Michael Clark . . . [et al.] ;
with a response by Mark R. Kowalewski ; edited by Michael L.
Stemmeler & J. Michael Clark.
    p. cm. -- (Gay men's issues in religious studies series ; v.
4)
Includes biblical references.
ISBN 0-930383-31-1 (pbk.) : $12.00
    1. Homosexuality--Moral and ethical aspects. 2. Homosexuality-
-Religious aspects. I. Clark, J. Michael (John Michael), 1953-
II. Kowalewski, Mark R., 1957-   . III. Stemmeler, Michael L.,
1955-   . IV. Series.
HQ76.25.G376 1993
176--dc20   93-22084
                                                 CIP

Gay Men's Issues in Religious Studies Series

under the general editorship of

J. Michael Clark & Michael L. Stemmeler

Forthcoming

in the

Gay Men's Issues
in
Religious Studies Series:

Volume 5

Proceedings
of the
Gay Men's Issues in Religion Group
of the
American Academy of Religion

San Francisco
Fall 1992

Topics will include:

Gay Spirituality, AIDS,
and Ecclesiology
and
Families and Coalitions:
Lesbians and Gay Men Creating
New Patterns of Community

* * *

Table of Contents

Michael L. Stemmeler

Preface

During the weekend of October 9–11, 1992 Washington, D.C., became the site of a grand spectacle. The San Francisco NAMES Project Foundation organized the display of the AIDS Memorial Quilt in its entirety. More than 21,000 quilt panels were on display and about 3,000 more were added in the course of the weekend. The total display covered 15 acres and weighed close to 30 tons.

I was very fortunate to be able to witness the Quilt display together with my partner of 10 years. We were particularly fortunate to be two of the more than a quarter of a million people who visited Washington on that weekend since the October 1992 display marked probably the last time that the NAMES Project Foundation was able to work out the logistics of a total Quilt showing.

The number of individual Quilt panels may well stand around 26,000 by today. Each one of them represents a person whose life was claimed by the AIDS pandemic. I claim to say that the Quilt is able, in an especially powerful way, to present the human face of AIDS. As Gay people who have been more than just concerned about AIDS since its onset in 1981, we are used to AIDS death statistics as they are are published in the *Morbidity and Mortality Weekly Reports*. But we also know first hand that behind each figure in a statistical table rests the life of a human being who still affects many other people, friends and families, lovers and acquaintances.

We also have to keep in mind that for the foreseeable future the Quilt will continue to grow. All the panels displayed in Washington represent about 13% of the total number of lives lost to AIDS in the United States alone and a mere 2% of deaths due to AIDS worldwide. Despite the fact that the Quilt memorializes those who have died from AIDS and therefore becomes a gigantic tapestry of death, it is also a tapestry of love and joy, of remembrance of the good times and the hard times in many people's lives, in the lives of those who have dies from AIDS and in the lives of their loved ones and caregivers. All these thoughts and emotions went through my head when I saw the Quilt lying on the Washington Mall, basked in sunshine, between the Washington and Lincoln Memorials. I compared the prevailing atmosphere among the visitors to a large festival of joy and at the same time to a festival of grief. There was lots of laughter and there were lots of tears. Lovers, friends, and family members gathered at the memorial panel of their lost loved ones, exchanged memories and mourned together. And for once it seemed possible in the United States to transcend racial and class boundaries, to forget about sexual orientation discrimination and gender differences. At the Quilt, during the candlelight vigil on Saturday night, and at the Political Funeral on Sunday there was only one group of people in the spotlight of the capital city, people affected by AIDS who were interested in raising the consciousness of the entire nation and its leaders to the magnitude of AIDS and who were willing to do anything to bring about an end to this scourge.

It is in front of this backdrop of the AIDS Memorial Quilt that I am happy to present to you this volume on *Gay Affirmative Ethics*. The papers collected and published in this fourth volume of the *Gay Men's Issues in Religious Studies Series* represent the scope of work of the Gay Men's Issues in Religion Group in the AAR during the AAR's 1991 meeting in Kansas City, MO.

Gay Affirmative Ethics, of course will always elude comprehensive treatment. As historical beings we are constantly confronted by a changing world and we are perennially challenged to respond to the many changes that materialize around us. Our answers are never once–and–for–all. We have to adept, adjust, and sometimes even radically alter our perceptions of the world and those around us. The present volume captures a momentary glimpse on the world and the problems and issues that currently occupy our concern. The contributors to this volume on *Gay Affirmative Ethics* have stepped outside of the boundaries of gay apologetics. They have developed a fresh and provocative approach to ethics and ethical problems as they are faced by Gay people. Departure point for these discourses on Gay ethics is—again rooted in proven liberation–theologically influenced methodology—the position of "those marginalized by the dominant discourse on sexuality as it has been expressed in the Judaeo-Christian tradition."* It is my sincere hope that this volume assist our readers in identifying more closely areas in need of undivided ethical attention and that it help them formulate their own ethically justified responses.

Mt. Pleasant, Michigan
3 November 1992,
a day of promise
for the United States

---

* See the response by Mark R. Kowalewski, "Revisioning a Sexual/Social Ethic: An Ongoing Journey," in this volume, pp. 113-123.

I. Jeffrey Hopkins:

The Compatibility of Reason and Orgasm in Tibetan Buddhism: Reflections on Sexual Violence and Homophobia

1. Introduction

Much of world culture views reason and sexual pleasure to be antithetical and relegates the pleasure of orgasm to a baser level of the personality incompatible with the true and the good. This has lent intellectual justification to exaggerated attempts by some males to assert control over the "baser" self (1) by identifying women and, by extension, male homosexuals with these "base" passions and (2) by committing violent acts (including sex) against these lowly creatures. They do this to foster the self-delusion that sexual impulses are under the control of their "higher" self. In Tibetan Buddhist systems, however, there are hints of a compatible relationship between reason and orgasmic bliss in that developed practitioners seek to utilize the blissful and powerful mind of orgasm to realize the truth and the all-good ground of consciousness. The practice is based on an experientially founded tenet that the most profound, subtle, and powerful level of consciousness, the mind of clear light, manifests in intense orgasm and that it can be used to realize the truth in an unusually powerful and effective way. The suggestion is that the sense of bifurcation between reason and orgasmic bliss is the result of not appreciating the basic nature of mind.

Tibetan teachings that present a series of related levels of consciousness in which conceptual reasoning and orgasmic bliss are viewed as parts of a continuum contrast with the sense of radical separation that is present in some situations of sexual violence. Many strands of modern society, especially in the United States, are almost pathologically concerned with controlling others' private lives. Why is this? It seems to me that a single, complex person is being divided into radically separate higher and lower selves such that the so-called higher self is exalted in status even to the point of becoming disembodied. This radical division lays the groundwork for projection of the lower self onto others, especially women and male homosexuals, and consequent even brutal attempts at control. The brutality ranges from outright physical violence to suppression of information about sex and sexual orientation such that our federal government even refuses to make information on sexual orientation available to teenagers who suffer a high rate of suicide due to conflicts related with sexual identity.

It is indeed an estranged society that fears knowledge of the actual practices of its members; the ludicrous perspective that is suggested by this situation is that of the "sodomy delusion", that is to say, if seemingly "straight" men tasted only once the joys of homosexual sex, they would be so enthralled that the halls of heterosexuality would be emptied, rather than a mere ten-percent defection. One gets the sense that the only way that the advocates of silence feel that heterosexual mores can be sustained is through the maintenance of ignorance, a state not of bliss but of pained projection of temptation onto others. Women and male homosexuals are viewed as tempting otherwise decent persons into their lower selves. Consider the fears that many have of gay teachers, who are seen as ready not only to convert but to misuse their students; the fears, however, are ridiculous in the face of the statistics on sexual abuse by teachers, the overwhelming majority being by heterosexual men. It does not take much profundity to surmise that those who favor ignorance about sexual matters have separated themselves from aspects of their own sexual impulses and, like the paranoiac, are pursued by images of libidinous attackers who are actually manifestations of their own minds.

Our acculturation is often so much at odds with our inner selves that we seek somehow to separate from our own inner being. Also, the external demands to identify with the current presentation of what is socially acceptable are so great that the tendency toward separation becomes institutionalized through peer-group fortification such that the attempt to separate oneself from one's own inner being becomes even more encrusted and difficult to penetrate. It is helpful in such situations to be confronted with systems of therapy that undermine the sense of separation from one's own inner self by uncovering the mechanisms of projection. It is also helpful to reflect on systems of structural psychology that place seemingly unassociated and radically other states of mind in a coherent continuum of mind such that the intellectual justifications for projection are undermined. I find one such system in various teachings found in Tibetan Buddhism, which, although by no means a panacea, offers stimulating food for thought.

2. *Background*

Buddhism began gradually to be introduced to Tibet in the seventh century C.E., more than a thousand years after Shakyamuni Buddha's passing away (*circa* 483 B.C.). The form Buddhism took in Tibet was greatly influenced by the highly developed systemization of the religion that was present in India through the twelfth century (and even later). The geographic proximity and relatively undeveloped culture of Tibet provided conditions for extensive transfer of scholastic commentaries and systems of practice, which came to have great influence throughout a vast region stretching from Kalmuck Mongolian areas in Europe where the Volga River empties into the Caspian Sea, Outer and Inner Mongolia, the Buriat Republic of Siberia, Bhutan, Sikkim, Nepal, and Ladakh. My sources are drawn primarily, but not exclusively, from one of the most scholastic orders of Tibetan Buddhism, the Ge-luk-ba[1] sect, founded by the polymath and yogi Dzong-ka-ba[2] (1357-1419) who was born in the northeastern province of Tibet called Am-do,[3] included by the occupying Chinese not in the Tibetan Autonomous Region but in the Ch'ing-hai Province. Dzong-ka-ba and his followers established a system of education centered in large universities, eventually in three areas of Tibet but primarily in Lhasa, the capital, which in some ways was as Rome is for the Catholic Church. For five centuries, young men (yes, women were, for the most part, excluded from the scholastic culture) came from all of the above-mentioned regions to these large Tibetan universities to study; until the Communist takeovers, they usually returned to their own countries after completing their degrees. My presentation will be largely from standard Ge-luk-ba perspectives[4] on the Tantra Vehicle, also called the Vajra Vehicle,[5] one of two basic forms of what Tibetan tradition accepts as Shakyamuni Buddha's teaching.

3. The Fundamental Innate Mind of Clear Light in Highest Yoga Tantra

In this Indo-Tibetan system it is said that during orgasm the mind of clear light—the basis of all consciousness and the most subtle and powerful form of consciousness—manifests, albeit only unconsciously, even to the untrained.[6] The *Guhyasamaja Tantra,* a Highest Yoga Tantra that is parallel in importance to the *Kalachakra Tantra,* divides consciousnesses into the gross, the subtle, and the very subtle.[7] We are all familiar with the grosser levels of mind—the eye consciousness that apprehends colors and shapes, the ear consciousness that apprehends sounds, the nose consciousness that apprehends odors, the tongue consciousness that apprehends tastes, and the body consciousness that apprehends tactile objects. To understand the perspective of this school of Buddhist thought, it is important that these five be considered not just as sensations known by another, separate consciousness, but as five individual consciousnesses that have specific spheres of activity—colors and shapes, sounds, odors, tastes, and tactile objects. These five sense consciousnesses are the grossest level of mind.

More subtle than the five sense consciousnesses but still within the gross level of mind is the usual, conceptual, mental consciousness. In Highest Yoga Tantra, these conceptions are detailed as of eighty types, divided into three classes. The first group of thirty-three is composed of emotions, feelings, and drives that involve a strong movement of energy [8] to their objects. Included in this group are fear, attachment, hunger, thirst, shame, compassion, acquisitiveness, and jealousy. The second group of forty conceptions involve a medium movement of energy to their objects; among them are joy, amazement, excitement, desiring to embrace, generosity, desiring to kiss, desiring to suck, pride, enthusiasm, vehemence, flirtation, wishing to donate, heroism, deceit, tightness, viciousness, non-gentleness, and crookedness. The third group of seven conceptions involve a weak movement of energy to their objects—forgetfulness, error as in apprehending water in a mirage, catatonia, depression, laziness, doubt, and equal desire and hatred. Although the difference between the first two groups is not obvious (at least to me), it is clear that in the third group the mind is strongly withdrawn; the three represent, on the ordinary level of consciousness, increasingly less dualistic perception.

Either through meditative focusing on sensitive parts of the body or through undergoing uncontrolled processes as in orgasm or in dying,[9] the currents of energy that drive the various levels of gross consciousness are gradually withdrawn, resulting in a series of altered states. First, one has a visual experience of seeing an appearance like a mirage; then, as the withdrawal continues, one successively "sees" an appearance like billowing smoke, followed by an appearance like fireflies within smoke, then an appearance like a sputtering candle[10] when little wax is left, and then an appearance of a steady candle flame. This series of visions sets the stage for the withdrawal of all conceptual consciousnesses,[11] whereupon a more dramatic phase begins the manifestation of profound levels of consciousness that are at the core of all experience.

The first subtle level of consciousness to manifest is the mind of vivid white appearance. All of the eighty conceptions have ceased, and nothing appears except this slightly dualistic vivid white appearance; one's consciousness itself turns into an omnipresent, huge, vivid white vastness. It is described as like a clear sky filled with moonlight, not the moon shining in empty space but space filled with white light. All conceptuality has ceased, and nothing appears except this slightly dualistic vivid white appearance, which is one's consciousness itself.

When, through further withdrawal of the energy that supports this level of consciousness, it no longer can manifest, a more subtle mind of vivid red or orange appearance (called increase) dawns. One's consciousness itself has turned into this even less dualistic vivid red or orange appearance; nothing else appears. It is compared to a clear sky filled with sunlight, again not the sun shining in the sky but space filled with red or orange light.

One's consciousness remains in this state for a period, and then when this mind loses its support through further withdrawal of the energy that is its foundation, a still more subtle mind of vivid black appearance dawns; it is called "near-attainment" because one is close to manifesting the mind of clear light. One's consciousness itself has turned into this still less dualistic, vivid black appearance; nothing else appears. The mind of black vastness is compared to a moonless, very dark sky just after dusk when no stars are seen. During the first part of this phase of utter blackness, one remains conscious but then, in a second phase, becomes unconscious in thick darkness.

Then, when the mind of black appearance ceases, the three "pollutants"[12] of the white, red/orange, and black appearances have been entirely cleared away, and the mind of clear light dawns. Called the fundamental innate mind of clear light,[13] it is the most subtle, profound, and powerful level of consciousness. It is compared to the sky's own natural cast—without the "pollutions" of moonlight, sunlight, or darkness—which can be seen at dawn before sunrise.

Because the more subtle levels of consciousness are considered to be more powerful and thus more effective in realizing the truth, the systems of Highest Yoga Tantra seek to manifest the mind of clear light by way of various techniques. One of these methods is blissful orgasm because, according to the psychology of Highest Yoga Tantra, orgasm involves the ceasing of the grosser levels of consciousness and manifestation of the more subtle, as do dying, going to sleep, ending a dream, sneezing, and fainting. The intent in using a blissful, orgasmic mind in the spiritual path is to manifest the most subtle level of consciousness, the mind of clear light, and use its greater power and hence effectiveness to realize the truth of the emptiness of inherent existence. The theory is that the apprehension that phenomena exist inherently or from their own side is the root of suffering because it induces the plethora of counter-productive emotions that produce suffering. In orgasm, phenomena that are over-concretized such that they seem to have their own independent existence melt into the expanse of the reality behind appearances. The pleasure of orgasm is so intense that the mind becomes totally withdrawn and fascinated such that both the usual conceptual mind and the appearances that accompany it melt away, leaving basic reality.

Through consciously experiencing this process, one can realize that ordinary conceptions and appearances are over-concretized. Sex, therefore, can become a practice through which this exaggeration of the status of appearance and mind is identified and subsumed in the source state. The fundamental state—which dawns in conscious orgasm—is not a dimming of the mind into an emotional state that is opposed to the truth, although it is often experienced as such because all of the usual conceptual minds are withdrawn during it. Rather, it is the basis of phenomena—that into which all appearances dissolve and thus the foundation of appearance. It is the reality behind appearances. Our unfamiliarity with it causes its implications to be missed in uncon-sciousness. Through developing realization of the emptiness of inherent existence by recognizing the inter-relatedness of persons and phenomena and through developing great compassion by recognizing relatedness over the continuum of lifetimes, one can become closer to this state and thereby more capable of appreciating its significance.

By utilizing this subtle level of mind, the power of the wisdom-consciousness realizing the truth is enhanced such that it is more effective in overcoming what prevents liberation from the round of rebirth and all its suffering. Such a wisdom consciousness is also more effective in overcoming what prevents knowledge of others' dispositions and of the techniques that can benefit them and thus serves to further the altruistic goals that are behind the quest for wisdom.

Sexual expression, therefore, can be used as an avenue for exploring the profound nature of consciousness which eventually brings release from craving from the root. Using an ancient example, the process is compared to a worm's being born from moist wood and then eating the wood. In this example (formed at a time when it was assumed that a worm or bug was generated only from wood and heat), the wood is desire; the worm is the blissful consciousness; and the consumption of the wood is the blissful consciousness's destruction of desire through realizing emptiness. As the First Pan-chen Lama, Lo-sang-chö-gyi-gyel-tsen,[14] says:[15]

> A wood-engendered insect is born from wood but consumes it completely. In the same way, a great bliss is generated in dependence on a causal motivation that is the desire of gazing, smiling, holding hands or embracing, or union of the two organs. The wisdom of undifferentiable bliss and emptiness, which is this great bliss generated undifferentiably with a mind cognizing emptiness at the same

time, consumes completely the afflictive emotions—desire, ignorance, and so forth.

Through desirous activities such as gazing at a loved one, or smiling, holding hands, embracing, or engaging in sexual union, a pleasurable consciousness is produced; it is used to realize the truth of the emptiness of inherent existence, whereby desire itself is undermined. The pleasurable consciousness is generated simultaneously with a wisdom consciousness, and thus the two are indivisibly fused. Without desire, the involvement in the bliss consciousness would be minimal, and thus Highest Yoga Tantra makes use of the arts of love-making to enhance the process.

In Ge-luk-ba texts, the undifferentiability of bliss and realization of emptiness is explained conceptually in terms of subject and object even though it is beyond all dualism. The bliss consciousness is the subject that realizes emptiness as its object. The reason for making this distinction is to emphasize that the bliss consciousness is used to realize the profound nature of reality, the emptiness of inherent existence—the emptiness of over-concretization—and thus is not a mere unconscious mind of orgasm. The aim of the sexual yoga is, therefore, not mere repetition of an attractive state but revelation of the basic reality underlying appearances. Nevertheless, to experience the union of bliss and emptiness, sexual pleasure has to be developed in fullness, and to do this it is necessary to implement techniques for avoiding premature ejaculation and extending the experience of pleasure; otherwise, a valuable opportunity is lost in the ephemerality of orgasm. The twentieth century Tibetan intellectual, Gedün Chöpel,[16] who traveled to India and wrote his own *Treatise on Passion* [17] based on the *Kama Sutra,* advocates the usage of sexual pleasure to open

oneself to the profound, fundamental state at the core
of all consciousness. As he says:

> The small child of intelligence swoons in
> the deep sphere of passion.
> The busy mind falls into the hole of a
> worm.
> By drawing the imaginations of
> attachment downwards
> Beings should observe the suchness of
> pleasure.

> Wishing to mix in the ocean of the bliss
> of the peaceful expanse
> This wave of magician's illusions
> separated off
> By perceiving the non-dual as dual,
> subject and object,
> Does one not feel the movement and
> igniting of the coalesced!

Phenomena that are over-concretized such that they
seem to have their own independent existence are
burnt away in the expanse of the reality behind
appearances:

> If one really considers the fact that the
> one billion worlds of this world system
> Are suddenly swallowed into a gigantic
> asteroid devoid of perception or feeling,
> One understands that the realm of great
> bliss
> Is that in which all appearances dissolve.

Gedün Chöpel also speaks of deities that are present
in the body during sex:

> At the time of pleasure the god and
> goddess giving rise to bliss actually dwell
> in the bodies of the male and the female.
> Therefore, it is said that what would be
> obstacles to one's life if done [under

usual circumstances] are conquered, and
power, brilliance, and youth blaze forth.
The perception of ugliness and dirtiness
is stopped, and one is freed from
conceptions of fear and shame. The deeds
of body, speech, and mind become pure,
and it is said that one arrives in a place of
extreme pleasure.

The question is *how* to sustain sexual pleasure so
that its spiritual value is not lost and the experience
turns into an unconscious dimming of mind. He
proposes forgoing cultural prohibitions so that sexual
pleasure can be deepened and extended such that it
penetrates the entire physical structure. With lyric
beauty he advises that inhibitions be cast aside:

Smear honey on each other and taste.
Or taste the natural fluids.
Suck the slender and bulbous tube.
Intoxicated and confusing the memory,
do everything.

As a technique to lengthen the experience of sexual
pleasure, he suggests pausing in the midst of intense
feeling and letting the feeling of bliss pervade the
body:

If one does not know the techniques of
holding and spreading the bliss that has
arrived at the tip of the jewel [i.e., the
head of the phallus], immediately upon
seeing it for a moment it fades and
disappears, like picking up a snowflake
in the hand. Therefore when, upon
churning about, bliss is generated, cease
movement, and again and again spread
[the sense of bliss throughout the body].
Then, by again doing it with the former
methods, bliss will be sustained for a
long time.

Through techniques of strengthening and lengthening sexual pleasure, both mind and body become bathed in bliss, opening the possibility of realizing the nature of the fundamental state.

The practice of sexual yoga is, to my knowledge, always explained in terms of heterosexual sex, in which a consort of the opposite sex[18] is used. The reason given concerns the structure of channels or nerves in the respective sexual organs, and thus insertion refers not just to insertion in the vagina but to contact with special nerve centers in the vagina that are lacking in the anus. Thus, colorful drawings of male and female deities in sexual union decorate the walls of temples—not those of same-sex couples. However, the type of sexual yoga that Gedün Chöpel describes has its foundations in the doctrine—found in the Old Translation School of Nying-ma[19]—that the blissful mind of clear light pervades all experience and is accessible within any state. This is the theoretical underpinning of his advice to extend the intense state of sexual bliss in order to explore the fundamental state of bliss. It seems to me that this *can* be done with same-sex or other-sex partners and *should* be done with whatever type is more evocative of intense feeling on all levels.

The ultimate goal is not just to experience this basal state into which phenomena have dissolved but also to perceive all the various phenomena of the world *within* the mind of clear light, without exaggerating their status into being independent. One is seeking to perceive interdependence without an overlay of divisive concretization. Emptiness does not negate phenomena; it negates only the exaggerated status of inherent existence and hence is compatible with love and compassion, which are enhanced through recognizing the connectedness of persons and of other phenomena. It is said that, with such a perspective, truly effective altruism is possible since the faculty of judgment is not clouded by afflictive emotions such as anger. The final state is not abstracted away from phenomena but is an appreciation of connectedness and embodiment. All phenomena are seen as manifestations of the mind of clear light, still having individuality but not exaggerated into being autonomous. Viewed in this perspective, the mind of orgasm as experienced in this type of sexual yoga is a means of linking to others, promoting intimacy and relationality, and is not an abstraction of oneself away from others into an auto-hypnotic withdrawal although it might seem so at first.

To summarize: The innermost level of consciousness is the fundamental innate mind of clear light, which is identified as the eighth in a series of increasingly subtle experiences that occur frequently but unconsciously in ordinary life. These deeper levels of mind manifest during the process of dying, going to sleep, ending a dream, fainting, sneezing, and orgasm in forward order:

1 mirage
2 smoke
3 fireflies
4 flame of a lamp
5 vivid white mind-sky
6 vivid red or orange mind-sky
7 vivid black mind-sky
8 clear light.

These eight also manifest in reverse order when taking rebirth, waking, starting to dream, ending a fainting spell, ending a sneeze, and ending orgasm:

1 clear light
2 vivid black mind-sky
3 vivid red or orange mind-sky
4 vivid white mind-sky

5   flame of a lamp
6   fireflies
7   smoke
8   mirage.

These states of increasing subtlety during death, orgasm, going to sleep, ending a dream, and so forth and of increasing grossness during rebirth, post-orgasm, awakening, beginning a dream, and so forth indicate levels of mind on which every conscious moment is built. From the perspective of this system of psychology, we spend our lives in the midst of thousands of small deaths and rebirths.

Conceptual over-concretization of objects prevents realization of the most profound and ecstatic state by generating attachment to superficial, unreal exaggerations. This attachment, in turn, fosters an inability to sustain the basic, blissful state that undermines emotionally imbedded self-deceptions. The suggestion is that ordinary conscious life is concerned with only the gross or superficial, without heed of more subtle states that are the foundation of both consciousness and appearance. We know neither the origin of consciousness nor the basis into which it returns.

It is said that ordinary beings are so identified with superficial states that the transition to the deeper involves even fear of annihilation; when the deeper states begin to manifest and the superficial levels collapse, we panic, fearing that we will be wiped out and, due to this fear, swoon unconsciously. As the late eighteenth and early nineteenth century Mongolian scholar Ngak-wang-kay-drup[20] says in his *Presentation of Death, Intermediate State, and Rebirth,*[21] at the time of the clear light of death ordinary beings generate the fright that they will be annihilated.[22] Similarly, the emergence of the foundational state in orgasm is so drastically different from ordinary consciousness that it is usually experienced as a dimming of the mind.

The fact that the mind of clear light—which is so awesome when it newly manifests—is one's own final nature suggests that the otherness and fear associated with its manifestation are not part of *its* nature but are due to the shallowness of untrained beings. The strangeness of our own nature is a function of misconception, specifically our mistaken sense that what are actually distortions of mind subsist in the nature of mind. We identify with these distortions such that when basic consciousness starts to manifest either in orgasm or in dying, we are unable to remain with the experience. The more we identify with distorted attitudes, the greater the fear of the foundational state, which to those who are trained has within it a source of sustenance beyond the dualism of subject and object. The systems of religious education found in the Tibetan cultural region can be viewed as aimed at overcoming this fear of one's most basic nature.

4. Reason and Orgasm

Although all consciousnesses arise from and return to the mind of clear light, the conceptualization that these grosser levels have their own independent existence causes these states to be alienated from their own source. In this Buddhist system, reason is a form of consciousness that in ordinary life is estranged from its own nature. Far from further fortifying the seeming separateness of reason through theorizing that such estrangement is a virtue, practitioners are called to try to perceive the inner nature of all states of mind, harmonious with the ground-state that can, through yogic training, be experienced consciously in orgasm. Not only the doctrines of structural psychology in Tibetan Buddhism but also the paintings and statutes of male and female in sexual union and of ithyphallic males that abound in Tibetan temples convey the message that the state of the all-good is harmonious with orgasm.

From this point of view, reason is gross in relation to orgasmic bliss, and when reason is considered a disembodied phenomenon, it is arrogant in its sense of distance from its own source-state. Under such circumstances the continuity between orgasm and conceptual consciousnesses such as reason is not being realized. It is my contention that this Indo-Tibetan perspective of continuity could help to alleviate the sense of loathing that some males experience with respect to the power that sexual pleasure has over them, when the surface personality is collapsed in orgasm and the panic of annihilation sets in. Fearing the destruction of the seemingly controlled self, they project their sexual impulses onto others, especially women and gay men— because they seem to wallow in sex and tempt them into their lower selves. Male homosexuals are threatening also because they are seen as males who approach sex, not from an overweening need for control but out of intimacy. Little do these people know that homophobic attitudes that block intimacy are also rampant among gays. As all of us, gay and non-gay, have seen, there is a strong tendency in some males to hate the sexual recipient, whether this be a woman or a man, as the source of their degeneration into an uncontrollable state. They attempt to assert control and dominion over the collapse and annihilation of their usual ego through hating the source of their sexual desire which they project onto others—these others being persons who are attracted to males. They seek domination both of their own sexual craving and also of the process of dissolution—in orgasm—of what is actually their superficial self. Panicking at their own disappearance in orgasm, they look for someone else to blame and to control even in brutal ways in order to distance themselves from their own craving for orgasm. At once attracted to and repelled by their own inner nature, they lash out in distorted disgust, attempting to claim a privileged position over a process that does indeed undermine their identification with superficial states. What is actually an exaggeration of a superficial state tries to pretend control over its profound source.

It seems to me that gay-bashing often arises from the tension of such persons' being faced (sometimes in fact but mostly in their imagination) with males who have not adopted this ridiculous projection. The Indo-Tibetan perspective that conceptual thought and orgasmic bliss have the same inner nature and that, in fact, the state of orgasmic bliss is more subtle than conceptual thought might help to undermine the warped need to attack homosexuals out of fear that they have not assumed the "proper" male perspective of dominance.

I do not mean to suggest that in these Indo-Tibetan systems reason is discarded, for it is highly valued as a means to open oneself to greater compassion and increased wisdom and, thereby, to break down the barriers to the conscious manifestation of the mind of clear light. However, the usefulness of reason becomes impossible when it exaggerates its own status into that of an independent, disembodied faculty, a process which promotes projection of other aspects of the personality onto others. Once reason is separated out as an autonomous entity and once persons identify mainly with this disembodied faculty, it is all too easy to view states and impulses that are actually part and parcel of one's own mind as threateningly impinging from the outside. Fear and rejection of sexuality lead to projection of sexuality onto women and homosexuals and result in fear, rejection, and abuse of women and homosexuals. Conversely, the elevation, exaltation, glorification, and deification of women (though seldom of homosexuals) has the same root in denial of sexual passion.[23]

The perspective of this Tibetan system may be useful in counteracting this tendency of self-created separation, for it presents reason as compatible with orgasmic bliss not only because the mind of clear light that manifests in orgasm is the inner nature of all consciousnesses but also because reason can reveal the conflict between appearance and reality, and a mind of orgasm can realize this same truth with even more impact. In this way, the veil of the exaggerated concreteness that is superimposed on phenomena is lifted, and the all-good ground of consciousness can manifest. This system of spiritual development that places such a high value on orgasm, viewed as harmonious with reason, beckons us to recognize the inner continuity of these seemingly separate states, thereby helping to undermine the pernicious processes of projection.

Let me be clear that I am not holding Tibetan culture up as a problemless model, a Shangri-La of sexual and social harmony and tolerance. Rather, I am suggesting that the model of consciousness found in Tibetan systems may be helpful in alleviating the estrangement of levels of the personality. Such a revolution in perspective requires recognition of vulnerability and thus is not easy. Perhaps, reflection on this Tibetan presentation of the connection between conceptual, reasoned levels of consciousness and the powerful state of orgasm may be useful for *both* non-homosexuals and homosexuals since the intellectual justifications that support homophobia are not limited to those who identify themselves as heterosexual.

¹ *dge lugs pa.*

² *song kha pa blo bzang grags pa.*

³ *a mdo.*

⁴ Given the emphasis within the Ge-luk-fla sect not just on separate monastic universities but even more so on individual colleges and given the general provincialism of the culture, it might seem impossible to speak of "standard" postures of the sect, but my meaning here points to generally recognizable, or at least representative, explanations.

⁵ *rdo rje theg pa, vajrayana.*

⁶ The section on the fundamental innate mind of clear light is adapted from my "A Tibetan Perspective on the Nature of Spiritual Experience", in *Paths to Liberation*, edited by Robert Buswell and Robert Gimello (Honolulu: U. of Hawaii Press, 1992).

⁷ The material on the levels of consciousness is drawn from Lati Rinbochay's and my translation of a text by A-gya-yong-dzin (*a kya yongs 'dzin*, alia Yang-jen-ga-way-lo-drö (*dbyangs can dga' ba'i blo gros*); see our *Death, Intermediate State, and Rebirth in Tibetan Buddhism* (London: Rider and Co., 1979; rpt. Ithaca: Snow Lion Publications, 1980).

⁸ Literally, wind or air (*rlung, prana*).

⁹ The similarity between orgasm and death in terms of seeming self-extinction is frequently noticed in "Western" literature, Shakespeare being the most prominent.

¹⁰ Literally, a butter-lamp.

¹¹ The three sets of conceptions correspond to the three subtle minds that appear serially after conceptions cease, but it is not that the three sets of conceptions cease serially; rather, they disappear together, resulting in the gradual dawning of the three subtler levels of mind.

¹² *bslod byed.*

¹³ *gnyug ma lhan cig skyes pa'i 'od gsal gyi sems.*

¹⁴ *blo bzang chos kyi rgyal mtshan.*

¹⁵ *Presentation of the General Teaching and the Four Tantra Sets*, Collected Works, vol. IV, 17b.5-18a.1.

¹⁶ *dge 'dun chos 'phel*; 1905-1951.

¹⁷ See Gedün Chöpel, *Tibetan Arts of Passion*, translated and introduced by Jeffrey Hopkins (Ithaca: Snow Lion Publications, 1992), from which I have drawn some of the material in this article.

[18] The female is called "mother" (*yum*), and the male is called "father" (*yab*). The terms are rich with suggestions (never made explicit in the tradition) of copulating with one's parent; it would seem that for heterosexuals this would be with the parent of the opposite sex, and for homosexuals, with the parent of the same sex.

[19] *rnying ma.*

[20] *ngag dbang mkhas grub*; 1779-1838. Also known as *kyai rdo mkhan po.*

[21] *skye shi bar do'i rnam bzhag*, Collected Works (Leh: S. Tashigangpa, 1973), Vol. 1, 466.2. Cited in Lati Rinbochay and Jeffrey Hopkins, *Death, Intermediate State, and Rebirth in Tibetan Buddhism* (London: Rider, 1979), p. 47.

[22] The fear-inspiring aspect of its manifestation accords with the often described awesomeness and sense of otherness that much of world culture associates with types of profound religious experience.

[23] Most of this sentence is not my own, but I do not remember where I found it.

II. Yoel H. Kahn

Making Love as Making Justice: Towards a New Jewish Ethic of Sexuality*

1.

The contemporary question "What does Judaism say about homosexuality?" does not lend itself to a simple answer. In accordance with Jewish tradition, I can best answer this question with another question or two: Which Judaism do you mean—biblical, rabbinic, medieval, pre-modern or modern? How can ancient sources speak to us about a category of meaning unconceptualized in their language and culture?[1] And if many contemporary Jews do not endorse the historical Jewish condemnation of male homosexual behavior, which, to be sure, is the unequivocal voice of the received tradition, what is our relation to the rest of historical Jewish teaching on human sexuality? How do we describe the logarithm of change which permits us simultaneously to dissent radically from received teaching while claiming to stand in and even represent the tradition from which it comes?

The full exploration of these questions is beyond the scope of this essay. I begin with these questions, though, in order to locate this essay within its larger context. This essay has its roots in an inquiry about Judaism and homosexuality[2] and in turn led to research on what liberal Judaism has had to say about human sexuality in general.[3] Ultimately, this inquiry led to an exploration of the theological self-understanding of how we mediate between the conflicting values of our received religious tradition and the contemporary society, a society of which we are both a part and have helped create. In this essay, a precis of a longer work in process, I shall outline how such a process might proceed by applying a methodology of liberal Jewish decision making to sexuality in general.[4]

2.

The starting place for any Jewish discussion of contemporary standards is historical Jewish teaching, as codified in the *halachah*, traditional Jewish law. Rooted in the Hebrew Bible and formulated in the Talmud, *halachah* has continued to evolve over the generations. The *halachah* about human sexuality is expressed in the context of the ancient rabbis' understanding of anthropology and physiology, and reflects their ideas about subjects as varied as authority, "natural law" and revelation as expressed through the Torah. None the less, we can posit five specific organizing values of sexuality within rabbinic culture. Although not always recognized by the rabbis, these organizing values give shape to—and account for much of—the *halachah* which defines appropriate sexual expression. These five values are: the economy of seed, the procreative purpose of sex, the role of women, *onah* (conjugal duty), and the concern for ritual purity.[5] The application of these values, within the wider context of the rabbinic world view and its concretization in the halachic system as a whole, generate the rules which regulate when and how sexual relations can occur. These rules are codified as *mitzvot*—sacred obligations. All the individual *mitzvot* are fulfilled out of the Jew's commitment to the covenant between God and Israel. The proper expression of sexual relations, as codified in the relevant *mitzvot*, is a significant aspect of a life of holiness in the covenant. We begin with a brief look at these five organizing rabbinic values and how they shaped sexual behavior.

The biblical and rabbinic traditions express abhorrence at the "destruction" of semen. In the ancient Near East, semen was considered a "life-force," akin to blood.[6] Apparently, people believed that there was a finite quantity of semen which could not be wasted. Further, as a "life-force" fluid, it had to be properly cared for and disposed of; and only acceptable repository for semen was inside a woman's vagina during intercourse. This concern for the quantity and disposition of seed is the primary basis for the later halachic prohibitions on male masturbation,[7] non-vaginal intercourse and coitus interruptus,[8] and the use of condoms[9] or diaphragms.[10]

Although pleasure and intimacy are known and legitimate aspects of rabbinic sexuality, the halachah has an overwhelming bias towards procreation.[11] Procreation is an affirmative *mitzvah* for men and, according to Talmudic law, a woman who is barren after ten years can be divorced by her husband.[12]

On the other hand, the halachah permits marriages and sexual relations which are known in advance to be infertile. The symbolic bias towards procreation is reflected in the halachah's permission of sexual intimacy with an infertile woman as long as the particular sexual act would be potentially procreative were the wife not infertile.[13] In general, the halachah only considers sexual acts which are *presumably* procreative licit.[14]

The wife's sexual role is determined in part by her second-class legal status in the *halachah.* The organizing premise of the *halachah* on marital relations is that a woman's sexual and reproductive capacities are the property of her husband.[15] Thus, there is a general rabbinic principle that "the husband may do as he pleases" with his wife. This value is in conflict with the rabbinic understanding of women's sexual needs and the husband's conjugal obligation.

This conflict is a source of tension throughout the generations.

A husband is obligated to have sexual relations with his wife at regular times. The biblical term *onah* (Exodus 21:11) is understood to mean conjugal rights. The 2nd century code the Mishnah specifies the frequency with which *onah* must be provided; later commentators differ as to whether these times constitute a minimum or maximum requirement. The rabbis expand the *mitzvah* to encompass the husband's obligation to provide sexual satisfaction to his wife.[16] The man's own sexual pleasure is not recognized by the halachah as a legitimate goal; the ancient rabbis saw men's sexual energy as boundless and in need of "control" while women's is more subdued and therefore must be aroused.[17] The regulation of sexual behavior is extended by some of the ancient rabbis to include approved and discouraged positions.

Finally, according to the halachah, sexual relations are forbidden during times of ritual impurity. A women is ritually unclean for up to fifteen days of each menstrual cycle,[18] during mourning and on other days on the personal and communal calendar.

The above organizing values underlie the halachic norms for licit sexuality. Summarizing these values and the behavorial norms they generate, the *halachah* teaches that sexual relations are licit and sacred when they occur:

1) between opposite sex-partners [19];
2) in the context of marriage[20];
3) through vaginal intercourse
   a) preferably in the missionary position
4) at permitted times according to the
religious calendar
5) at permitted times during the women's
menstrual
6) with attention to the women's satisfaction
and pleasure[21]

7) with the expectation that the act will be procreative.[22]

3.

The above criteria reflect the halachah's specific understanding of sexuality on the micro level, and, on the macro level, are consistent with the entirety of the halacha's world-view. Our modern response properly begins, therefore, with an acknowledgement that our organizing values are different than those of our ancestors, reflecting our changed priorities and premises. These values are grounded in our contemporary understanding of the meaning of God, Torah and Israel. They emerge out of our ongoing dialogue with God, out of historical Jewish teaching, and out of the lived experience of the Jewish people, men and women, gay and non-gay, as the embodiment of contemporary Jewish culture, itself embedded in liberal Western culture. Before turning to the specific question of sexuality, let's first note some of the organizing values of contemporary liberal Judaism and point out how they shape a modern Jewish ethic of sexuality.

The Torah teaches us that each person—as person—is created in the divine image. We first part from previous generations when we place particular emphasis on the ultimate dignity of the person and the individual's autonomy as part of the blessing of being made in the divine image. Accordingly, we explicitly reject Judaism's historical distinction between men and women and insist upon complete equality for all individuals. Second, we lift up the human capacity for relationship as an especially significant aspect of humanity's creation in the divine image. Martin Buber is our primary teacher of this value.

Our sexual lives and sexual relationships should not be separated from the rest of our lives and relationships, but part of a continuum with them. Applying our organizing values of personal dignity, equality and relationship to the realm of sexuality, we believe that sexuality, at its core, is a yearning for connectedness, intimacy and relationship. Sexual intimacy, an expression of intimate human meeting, can be a route to and expression of "knowing" another, to borrow from Hosea, "in justice, in truth and in faithfulness."[23] It can therefore be a primary mode of both spirituality—knowing God, as Carter Heyward has taught, and of justice-making—making God known.[24]

Sexual intimacy is one place along an "intimacy continuum" and intimacy is a section of the "relationship continuum." The route to knowing God, says Buber, is through our relationships. If the route to knowing God is through knowing others, than our yearning for another and the seeking after intimacy, connectedness and relationship is a God-seeking act. The experience of knowing another with sexual intimacy can bring us closer to God. Just as our worship can be misdirected and result in idolatry, so can this yearning for intimacy and connection be misdirected in idolatrous ways.[25]

Our commitment to the equality, dignity and autonomy of each person as an individual is unprecedented in our tradition. We should not be surprised, therefore, that the *halachah*'s categories which strictly regulate permitted and forbidden acts do not satisfy our desire to affirm as much individual autonomy as possible. In general, we turn away from the *halachah*'s concern for the acceptability of discrete acts and instead emphasize the quality of the relationship in which the actions occur. We consider the possibility that any sexual acts—whether previously permitted or forbidden—can be a means to the realization of sanctified human relationship through sexual intimacy. Our most intimate relationships should be the place of our primary and greatest expression of covenantal justice. Our sexual lives are a significant opportunity for and important place of transformation of the ordinary and instinctual into the sacred.[26] Accordingly, our religious interpretation of sexuality is measured not according to whether acts are permitted or forbidden, nor ritually pure or impure, but whether the relationship as a whole and its specific expression is just or unjust, contributing to or diminishing from holiness.

Sexual relationship can be an expression of and seeking after covenantal relationship. Covenantal commitment is lived out over time and as part of a community. Our sexual relationships, when lived as aspects of covenantal living, are properly respectful of both of these commitments. Accordingly, we must consider the long term impact and possible consequences of our actions. Made in God's image, we need to consider our own selves. As part of our covenantal relationships, we should be equally concerned for our partners. Covenant living occurs within a community. Responsible sexual expression, therefore, occurs with attention to and respect for the existing commitments of both partners, whether these are commitments to themselves or to others.[27]

4.

How then do we understand received Jewish teaching on sexuality? We reconsider the organizing values—and their consequent embodiment in specific *mitzvot*—in light of our own organizing values and total world view. We begin with a bias towards affirming historical Jewish practice unless the organizing value or its application conflict with our contemporary organizing values. In order to affirm a primary value, it is sometimes necessary to modify, reinterpret or even reject a historical value and the *mitzvot* it generated. Let's return to the five organizing values of the rabbinic teaching on sexuality and consider them in light of our organizing values.

We begin with the ban on spilling seed. The physiological concerns for not wasting semen have been long answered by modern science. We no longer consider ourselves bound by the biblical and rabbinic prohibtions concerning the other life-force fluid, blood; is there any enduring spiritual value in maintaining in some form the ban on wasting semen? We do not think so; in fact, we consider acts which were formerly forbidden on this basis (e.g. masturbation) to be otherwise perfectly acceptable, and, in proper circumstances, even desirable.

Two, if the secondary status of women is a basic premise of the *halachah*, a central value for Reform Jews is the legal, covenantal and personal equality of women and men. This emerges from our valuation of every human being as a reflection of the divine image and our internalization of what we value in Western culture. A consequence of this organizing value is our rejection of any aspect of the tradition which discriminates between persons on the basis of gender.[28]

We affirm the traditional value of sexuality as a means of procreation, but we no longer accept procreation as the primary paradigm around which sexuality is organized. Instead, we will propose that covenantal relationship is the paradigm of sexual activity. If procreation is no longer the ontological paradigm, heterosexuality need no longer be the ideal mode of sexual expression.

In the halachic system, responsibility for another's sexual pleasure as a *mitzvah* is limited to the husband's obligations to his wife. Most halachic authorities hold that a married couple is permitted whatever sexual acts the husband desires regardless of the procreative potential of the act. Combining this traditional norm with our modern commitment to equality between persons, we expand the *mitzvah* of *onah* to include obligations of both partners to seek to satisfy the sexual needs of the other. We cannot accept the principle that "a man can do what he wishes" regardless of the woman's desires because it denies the woman's equality and autonomy. We transvalue this rabbinic teaching, and invoking our value of equality and mutuality in relationship, conclude that mutually desired sexual acts between two persons are acceptable, so long as the individual acts and the relationship as a whole meet the ethical criteria for right relationship and right action, as explained below.

The fifth value, the question of ritual purity, is so bound up with other aspects of the rabbinic system of daily life, that a full discussion is beyond the scope of this essay. Let us merely note that we treat the system of ritual purity as another potential route to spirituality whose demand can properly only be taken on by an individual and can no longer be imposed from without.

Earlier, we listed the criteria for licit sexual expression according to the *halachah.* The comparable list in our system begins in our understanding of sexual expression as a dimension of our covenantal relationship with God, in the context of and contributing to right relation. We believe that this is possible when sexuality is expressed:

> 1. between equals—people who are peers in maturity, independence, and personal and physical power
> 2. who share mutual respect and affection
> 3. who assume equal responsibility for the possible consequences of their sexual activity [29]
> 4. with concern for one another's pleasure

5. with concern for one another's physical and emotional health and well being
6. in the context of open communication and truth telling
7. with respect for one another's body right and bodily integrity.
8. in the context of and with attention to each person's existing personal and communal covenantal obligations to others.

The above, superficially dualistic presentation, between a modern focus on the context and relationship, in contrast to the tradition's emphasis on the specifics and circumstances of actions, distorts the nuances of both systems. Nonetheless we are indeed proposing a radical break with our tradition's teaching.

5.

Up to this point, we have not explicitly spoken about homosexuality. Male homosexual acts are forbidden by explicit biblical command and are condemned as violations of the prohibitions against spilling seed and non-procreative intercourse. In so far as these historical concerns are no longer in force as criteria for heterosexual behavior,[30] the continued application of them as a reason to condemn homosexual acts can only be considered homophobic. We do explicitly reject the biblical prohibition on homosexual acts, applying it its place our contemporary standard of covenant relationship, in which acts and actors are measured not in accordance of who and what they are but how they live.

6.

Some liberal Jewish teachers have cautioned against rejecting traditional values in favor of the prevailing cultural values of the society in which we live. It is appropriate, therefore, to explicitly note some of the ways in which our new Jewish ethic dissents from the prevailing cultural ethos which surrounds us. Although our new ethic is fundamentally a departure of Jewish tradition as seen through the prism of the organizing values of this generation of liberal Jews, it is also a corrective of the culture from which it emerges. We part from the mainstream of American culture in three notable ways: the focus on pleasure, the use of sexuality as an instrument of power, the genital focus of sexual expression.

American culture treats sexuality primarily as a form of personal pleasure. We consider pleasure desirable, as does the Jewish tradition. However, the excessive focus on personal pleasure and private ego-needs opens the door to the exploitation and abuse of others. Our concern with mutuality excludes a sexual ethic which ends with the self.[31]

The Jewish tradition, through the prophetic tradition, has always been concerned about the abuse of power. By and large, our concern has been with the use and abuse of power in the wider, social and political realm. Feminism has taught us to consider the place of power in interpersonal relationships as well. Just sexual relationships cannot occur when sexuality is used as an instrument of control or power. Nor is justice consistent with the use of power or its threat to coerce or force another into sexual intimacy.

Susan Brownmiller argues persuasively that in our culture violence is erotic and passion is associated with having power over another or being overpowered by another.[32] This attitude is supported by the cultural definition of sexual relations as "conquest." Our ethic of sexuality therefore includes the transformation of culture so that mutuality is erotic, personal empowerment is desirable and passion is linked to both strength and tenderness.[33] The understanding of sexual relations as an act of conquest, along with the historical emphasis on procreation, has led to the focus on genital sexuality. Contemporary cultural images of sexuality, whether in advertising or pornography, gay and straight, continue to equate sexual pleasure with genital contact. In contrast, when sexuality is an instrument of intimacy and relationship, than the total person and the total act will be eroticized. Such sexual expression changes the focus of the act from the goal (orgasm) towards the experience of mutual intimacy.

7.

If, as Buber taught, we come to know God through our I-Thou relationships with others, then our most intimate relationships with others are a unique place for sacred living. The I-Thou relationship demands that we see another not as an object but as a wholistic person in the divine image. Because we are so vulnerable in these private relationships, we are uniquely challenged to practice ethical living and covenant respect in our sexual lives. Through learning to live and act justly in this private sphere, and through the enhancement of our own person which emerges from true relationship, we are strengthened and encouraged to channel passion and action towards justice in wider, more public spheres. The realization of our most intimate yearnings is not a closed circle which in turn leads us back to our partner; rather, the Jewish dialectic of personal and communal obligation turns us outward from the most intimate sphere to return and reengage in the labor of restoring and healing the world.

* This paper is the product of a lengthy collaboration with my colleague, Rabbi Margaret Moers Wenig of Hebrew Union College-Jewish Institute of Religion, New York, who began this research and contributed the title, the structure and many of the ideas.

[1] Even if we limited our discussion to the contemporary Reform movement, the primary liberal wing of American Judaism, we would immediately discover a vast range of positions.

[2] Yoel H. Kahn, "Judaism and homosexuality: The traditional/progressive debate." *Journal of Homosexuality* 18:3-4 (1989/90), pp. 47-82; this essay appears in a slightly different form in *Homosexuality, the Rabbinate and Liberal Judaism* (New York, N.Y.: Central Conference of American Rabbis, 1989).

[3] The answer is "not much." The paucity of discussion illustrates, in my opinion, the uncomfortableness of the contemporary Jewish community with sexuality and confronting the chasm between the values of the halachah and those of this culture.

[4] See Kahn, 1989; Yoel H. Kahn, "The *kedushah* of homosexual relationships." *CCAR Yearbook XCIX* (New York, N.Y.: Central Conference of American Rabbis, 1989), pp. 136-141.

[5] The discussion which follows is based in large part on David Feldman's exhaustive research in *Marital relations, birth control and abortion in Jewish law* (New York, N.Y.: Schocken, 1974). The conclusions are, of course, my own.

[6] In the biblical world, blood and semen both ritually polluted those who came in contact with them. The force of the later rabbinic prohibition was greatly strengthened when the 13th century mystical book, the *Zohar*, declared the violation of this law "greater than all other transgressions." (*Zohar*, Va'yeshev, 188a). The Zohar's statement was codified in the later codes, including the very influential 16th century work, the *Shulchan Aruch* (E.H. 23). See Feldman, chap. 6. *passim*, esp. p. 115, n. 37 ff.

[7] Talmud, Niddah 13a; Moses Maimonides, *Mishnah Torah*, "Issurei Bi'ah (Laws of Forbidden Intercourse)" 21:18: "*K'ilu harag nefesh.*"

[8] See Feldman, pp. 152-154. On non-vaginal intercourse, see pp. 155 ff and below.

[9] See "Hashhatat Zerah" *Encyclopedia talmudit* (Jerusalem, Israel: Talmudic Encyclopedia Institute, 1965) vol. 11, col. 141, n. 179, and Feldman, pp. 229-230.

[10] See Feldman, Part IV, esp. pp. 227 ff. According to the stringent *poskim* (decisors), the concern for *shefichat zerah* prohibits all non-procreative sexual activity, including intercourse in which the semen is not directly deposited in the

vagina. See the responsum of the Asheri, *Teshuvot ha-Rosh,* Klal 33, no. 3, cited in Feldman, p. 153 and the discussion which follows, esp. p. 155, n. 60.

[11] This principle is articulated in the tannaitic statement: "If a man married a woman and remained with her for ten years and she has not yet given birth, he is not allowed to neglect further the duty of procreation." Talmud, Yevamot 64a and parallels. See Feldman, pp. 37-45. The rabbis did not require the husband to divorce his wife in practice; see the responsum cited in Feldman, p. 40, n. 104.

[12] Current *halachah* does not require a man to divorce an infertile wife.

[13] What is permitted to an fertile couple is permitted to an infertile couple and what is not permitted a fertile couple is likewise not permitted to an infertile couple. Feldman quotes *Nimmukei Yosef,* the 15th century commentary to Al-Fasi's code:

> *Intercourse* with a woman incapable at all of child-bearing is permissible, and the prohibition of *hash-hatat zerah* is not involved so long as the intercourse is in the manner of procreation; for the rabbis have in every case permitted *marriage* with women too young or too old for childbearing. No prohibition is involved with a barren or sterile woman, except that the mitzvah of procreation is not thus being fulfilled (Feldman, p. 68; emphasis in original).

[14] According to Feldman, p. 66, it is not particular non-procreative acts but "consciously fruitless marriage" that "so violates the very spirit of Judaism." According to the rabbis, the "natural" sexual act, is intercourse in the missionary position. Some authorities permit "unnatural acts" (woman on top, rear entry, anal intercourse), basing themselves on the talmudic passage: "A man may do with his wife as he will." Feldman, p. 155, n. 63. See Talmud, Nedarim 20b, Sanhedrin 58b, and Moshe Feinstein, *Igrot Moshe,* E. H., pp. 63-64, cited in Feldman, p. 165. Feldman comments: "Here we have an example of an act which, while sanctioned by law, was a source of embarrassment to the many moralists who could not bring themselves to accept so liberal a ruling even in theory. Unnatural positions are prohibited either on the basis of 'immorality' (*Shulchan aruch,* O.H. 240:5), or because they interfere with procreation (E.H. 25:2)." Many *poskim* who were inclined to permit "unnatural acts" on this basis felt constrained by the force of the Zohar's prohibition on *hash-hatat zerah* and its later codification. See *Encyclopedia talmudit,* esp. n. 139, which quotes a later commentator about a permissive ruling: "If he had seen what the Zohar says about the punishment of ... this [transgression], since it is greater than all of the other transgressions, than he would never have written what he did."

15 The husband [*ba'al*] "acquires" her from her father. This premise begins the mishnaic discussion of marriage: "A woman is acquired in one of three ways... (Mishnah, Ketubot 1:1). The talmudic discussion of this passage explores how marriage is both like and unlike property. See Rachel Biale, *Women and Jewish law* (New York, N.Y.: Schocken, 1984), pp. 46-49. The term *kedushah* in the context of marriage means "set aside" or "reserved" (See Biale, p. 48; Abraham Ibn-Shoshan, *Ha-Milon he-chadash* (Jerusalem, Israel: Kiryat Sefer, 1979) vol. 6, col. 2292, def. 2). In a divorce, the "setting aside" of the woman is reversed, as she moves from the special status of "reserved for a particular man" ("*mekudeshet li*") to the general "permitted to any man" ("*mooteret le kol adam*"). Adultery therefore is intercourse between a man and another man's wife. (Deut. 22:22; Talmud, Kiddushin 80b-81b; Biale, pp. 183-184; Epstein, *Sex laws and customs in Judaism* (New York, N.Y.: Ktav, 1967), pp. 196-199. Rape is considered a crime against property whose penalty was the monetary reimbursement of the value of the raped woman by the rapist to the woman's father (Deut. 21:28-29; Biale, p. 243).

16 Including, according to Moses Nachmanides, "physical intimacy, appropriate surroundings and regularity." Nachmandies on Ex 21:11, cited in Biale, p. 129.

17 Biale, 121-146 *passim,* esp. p. 137. Biale also discusses the rabbis' understanding of male and female sexual desire which shaped their norms of acceptable behavior.

18 The biblical basis for the laws of *niddah* is Leviticus 15:19-33. Their application was greatly expanded by the rabbis. A couples' freedom to enjoy sex and physical intimacy together is greatly restricted by the requirements of *niddah.* For a full discussion, see Biale, pp. 147-174.

19 The biblical and rabbinic world has not concept of "homosexuality." Male homosexual behavior is strictly forbidden in Leviticus 18. Lesbianism is also prohibited by the *halachah* but considered a less severe crime. See Maimondies, "Issurei Bi'ah," 1:14, 21:8, and Biale, pp. 192 - 194.

20 Intercourse between a man and a woman not forbidden to each other effected a marriage between them; such "marriages" were prohibited by the later authorities.

21 See Feldman, pp. 72-74 and esp. notes 78-82 there.

22 See Feldman, pp. 65 - 70.

23 Hosea 2:21.

24 Beverly Wildung Harrison, *Mzaking the conne ctions: Essays in feminist social ethics* Carol. S. Robb, ed., Boston, MA: Beacon, 1985, p. 149, quoted in Carter C. Heyward, Touching our strength: The erotic as power and the love of God (San Francisco, CA.; Harper and Row, 1989), p. 55.

---

[25] We consider the exploitation of sexuality and the treatment of people as sexual objects as primary forms of contemporary idolatry. We are aware of the vast potential for evil and abuse in the realm of sexuality and sexual power. While sexuality is not the only or exclusive route to intimacy and connectedness, its special place in the order of human need cannot be ignored or denied.

[26] This is our understanding of *kiddushin* - a sanctified relationship.

[27] Adultery, therefore, is properly understood as the violation of covenantal trust between two people.

[28] See, for example, the rjection of the ceremony for *pidyon ha-ben,* redemption of the first born son, in Simeon J. Maslin, ed. *Gates of mitzvah* (New York, N.Y.; Central Conference of American Rabbis, 1979), p. 72, n. 19.

[29] I.e., assume mutual responsibility for contraception, safer sex, emotional and material support for abortion, pregnancy, childbirth or offspring.

[30] If this were not so, than Jews would practice birth control in accordance with halachic, rather than Western, standards.

[31] This is a central theme in Borowitz, *Choosing a sex ethic* (New York, NY: Shocken, 1968). We particularly reject the mass cultural portrayal of casual sexual activity without attention or concern for either consequences or continuity.

[32] Susan Brownmiller, *Against our will: Men, women and rape* (New York, NY: Simon and Schuster, 1975), chap. 4.

[33] Carter Heyward and Beverly Harrison in a discussion at "Conference on What Women Theologians are Thinking," Union Seminary, New York, N.Y., October 1987.

III. J. Michael Clark
with Bob McNeir

Masculine Socialization and Gay Liberation: Excerpts

An Atlanta colleague has described me as a "curmudgeon" for our community.[1] I have grown to appreciate this label because I believe I turn my curmudgeonly evaluations upon myself as thoroughly as I do upon my community. And yet, as a curmudgeon, I know I ask difficult questions. As a gay liberation theologian, I believe that without asking ourselves difficult questions we will never achieve our fullest liberation. Gay and lesbian liberation is far more than mere sexual freedom, far more even than the achievement of certain political and legal rights and protections which are far too long in coming. Our liberation is something more fundamental than these things. To achieve our most complete and most genuine liberation will require the transformation of who we are—the transformation, the redemption if you will, of our very being. I know of no other way into and through this process than by way of confronting those things which keep us acquiescing and assimilating rather than radically transforming ourselves and the world. As a result, my reflections here, and the book project from which they are excerpted,[2] examine some of those things which inform our lives as gay men—specifically our masculine socialization—by way of the work of James Nelson and others.

Nelson writes that "no one can claim [absolute] sexual wholeness. Human beings live with deformities caused by fear and guilt, by the ravages of spiritualistic and sexist dualism, by sexual abuse and homophobia, by the curtains of silence and shame lowered even in this supposedly enlightened time."[3] In those same pages he goes on to suggest that part of our dilemma is our unfulfilled aching for "the redemption of our bodies" (Rom. 8:22-23). In examining alternatives to our patriarchal dilemma(s), Nelson subsequently acknowledges that sexual freedom is promising when it involves caring, tenderness, and mutuality or reciprocity. More often, however, in a deeply patriarchal culture, such supposedly liberated sexuality has instead "led many people to a frantic search for sensation, thence to the deadening of sensation [the satiation of promiscuity], and to erotic depersonalization."[4]

Since Stonewall a vast number of gay men, rebelling against all heteroconstraints, have plunged headlong into promiscuity with the result that they have become completely alienated from their sexuality and from their bodies themselves. Gay male sexuality has too often been reduced to the "mere bodily function" of orgasms, while the emptiness which such alienation and reductionism causes has produced a compulsive drive for more and more such experiences—truly a vicious cycle. Even after the initial shock of AIDS in our community, a new generation of gay men have discovered that "safe sex techniques" again enable a renewed, although presumably safer, promiscuity— AIDS notwithstanding. Granted, given the conditions of life for gay men prior to Stonewall and the development of gay liberation after 1969, that makes sense up to a point: When an essential part of who we are has been repressed for such a very long time, once that part of us is released, there is a kind of "making up for lost time" which naturally occurs. A very significant pent up part of ourselves as gay men finally got released. But, somewhere toward the end of the first decade of gay liberation, rather than being a psychologically healthy release, this flurry of sexual activity became self-perpetuating; it became an obsessive life-style, an end unto itself. What it meant to be gay had become nothing more than having more and more of what we thought we wanted. But that alone proved unfulfilling and diverted too many of us from pursuing other aspects of liberation.

One of the problems which has held us back in this way has been our enculturated fear of intimacy. Nelson has noted, for example, that "intimacy does not come easily [for men]. What seem[s] natural to men is that individuals are ultimately separate from each other."[5] For gay men this self vs. other separation works against us in at least three ways: (1) It undergirds, encourages, or certainly makes easier, anonymous sexual encounters wherein both partners are disengaged from each other, where the sexual exchange and the sexual partner are not integrated into one's sense of self. (2) Conversely, such enculturated duality, such practiced separation and alienation make genuine mutuality, reciprocity, and intimacy very difficult when two similarly enculturated gay men try to form a coupled relationship as spouses. (3) It may also encourage gay men to be loners, to be men detached from (and distrustful of) community and, hence, from the communal politics necessary for achieving liberation.

Associated with this isolated sense of self-apart is a male fear of self-disclosure. Separated men, gay or nongay, may always need to hold some part of themselves back, even in their seemingly most intimate relationships.[6] This fear of self-disclosure is really an umbrella fear which also includes fear of disapproval; fear of vulnerability; fear of emotions and feelings; and, fear of loss of control, of boundaries collapsing, of the walls of separated selfhood disintegrating. This web of fears and male insecurities clearly works against male same-sex friendships and intimacy. These enculturated fears are certainly serious obstacles to our achieving a healthy, wholistic sexuality based on a paradigm of friendship.[7] Nelson also notes the obvious male tendency "to separate sex from intimacy" and adds, "men can tolerate, even enjoy, impersonal sex more readily, for sexual feelings [retain] a somewhat independent status for them."[8] For gay men the separation of self from sexual feelings also gets reinforced by homophobia—by the heteropatriarchal rejection of gayself identity—which further encourages non-relational gay pro-miscuity. In other words, if we distance ourselves from our sexual behavior, if we do not allow ourselves to become emotionally involved with our sexual partners, then somehow we do not feel as thoroughly homosexual as when we are constantly confronted, every morning and every evening, by a same-sex mate. Promiscuous distance keeps our homosexuality itself from our full conscious awareness; "mere genital functions" prevent us from fully encountering, wrestling with, and accepting our thoroughgoing gay identities.

Ironically, this enculturated separation of sex from intimacy actually leads to a confusion of the two. Men seek sex when what they are really seeking is an intimacy seemingly denied them, as men. The separation of self from sexual feelings and feelings in general ironically means that "if a man feels intense emotions, sex seems called for."[9] In other words, the spectrum of emotions becomes conflated and subverted, mistakenly, into sexual feelings. Moreover, if intimacy and emotions constitute a threat to heteropatriarchal masculinity, same-sex affection becomes far more threatening than sexual behavior. The threat which nurtures homophobia is not homosexuality per se, but gay identity and affections. Gay men are certainly caught in a bind; as a result of the threat to our enculturated understanding of proper masculinity which same-sex intimacy in addition to homosexual behavior presents, too many of us have unreflectively rejected intimacy altogether, appeasing our own internalized and conflicted heterosexist self-images with an utter separation of our maleselves—our very being—from a compulsive and impersonal sexual promiscuity. One alternative may be to more honestly examine what motivates our sexual behavior: Why are we behaving the way we are? Why are we avoiding dealing with intimacy? Is an individual treating himself as a human being? Is he treating his partners as human beings, or just as sex objects? Or, is he avoiding the responsibility that entails?

Ultimately, James Nelson provides a number of analyses which, transposed into the experiences of gay men, can help us to penetrate and understand these and other dilemmas posed for us by traditional masculine socialization. For example, he notes that "boys are slower in developing positive body images than are girls, ... are less secure about their gender roles, and ... tend to cling to rigid and stereotypical concepts of masculinity," which, obviously, makes both gayself-acceptance and a healthy relational gaysexuality all the more difficult for gay men.[10] By the time we are adults, we "have lost touch with our vulnerability, our deepest human capacities for tenderness, our need for dependence—in short, a whole range of emotions. ... We are...alienated from our bodily existence, and our sexuality ... has taken a narrow genital focus."[11] Nelson subsequently provides a number of insights as to the problems caused by this genitalization of male sexuality. He observes that the masculine focus is traditionally on "sexual acts, acts involving genital expression. In turn, we tend to isolate [or separate] sex from other areas of our lives"; rather than embodying intimacy, playfulness, and communion, male sexuality is reduced to genital events, which also means "our sexual organs are highly important [including their size!] to our male self-images."[12] That our male genitals are "external, visible, and easily accessible to touch," something we experience as having a "mind of their own," only reinforces this obsession.[13] For gay men this general masculine externalization and genitalization of sex has made promiscuity virtually inevitable, from the accumulation of genital events and the personal dissociation of self from those events, to the subcultural obsession with genital size.

And yet, this genitalization does not stop with our troubled sexuality alone. It further reverberates throughout our being as men: "Male genitalization seems to encourage men to prize the qualities of hardness, upness, and linearity. ...The erection mentality [gets] projected upon the world and what seems to be valuable in it."[14] Valuing linear history and goal-directedness sets men in opposition to natural cycles, more associated with menstrual femininity. It pits "straight" (linear, erect) men against "unstraight" (bent, presumably receptive and effeminate) gay men. It pits performance and individual power and achievement (competition) against more democratic communal processes. It values domination more than cooperation. The linear, erection mentality behind and within masculinely socialized male sexuality has also produced certain stereotypes of what male sexuality is. None of these is particularly healthy for any man, gay or nongay: Malesex is goal-oriented and orgasmic; to be physically intimate implies a genital, orgasmic outcome. Malesex is performance-based; a man must always want and always be ready for sex. Malesex is controlling and dominating; the man is in charge, the sole initiator. Malesex depends upon competitive relating, fears vulnerability, and keeps other people (especially other men) at safe distance from the fragile up-linear self. Malesex entails problems with communi-cating or even understanding one's own emotions and an ever-nagging self-doubt as to whether one is masculine enough.

A related concern for Nelson, therefore, is that of male performance anxiety, the persistent male fear of never being good enough (hard enough, erect enough, powerful enough)—which can then "become symbolic of [all of] life beyond the direct sexual experience"; men are social-ized to perform— to be psychologically ever-erect—throughout life, such that "the fear of failure is always lurking in the wings. Then comes the temptation to express hostility toward those making the performance demands."[15] This complex of performance anxiety, of fear of failure, and of the resultant overcompensations, results in aggression toward anyone perceived as demand-ing—toward authority figures in the world or toward partners and spouses. Two gay men caught up in this unresolved complex of anxiety, demands, fears, and overcompensations are forever pitted against one another; a healthy sexuality and a whole, mutual relationship will remain ever-elusive for them. More recently, Nelson again describes the extent to which performance anxiety permeates the male psyche and gets projected onto the world: "The performance mode of life is always demanding, and failure always lurks in the shadows. Because it is a strenuous, anxious life, [we] get angry. And if ... genital performance has become symbolic of a whole way of life, at whom might [we] be angry?"[16] At our parents, as vehicles of our socialization? At our culture, for shaping us into this mold? Or, as gay men, at our partners and spouses, insofar as they are also themselves otherthreatening, competitive, performing, and up-striving, weapons-erect men? Obviously, performance anxiety (and its overcompensation, competition) can become "a whole way of life. And it involves a high degree of self-consciousness, self-judgment, and fear of derision from others,"[17] all of which fosters low self-esteem and mitigates against self-acceptance. We have all, especially we gay men, somehow gotten the message that nothing we can do is ever good enough or erect enough.

Among the ways in which we can break the power of our socialization is to relearn relational values—essentially to reprogram ourselves for entering into, nurturing, and sustaining relationships. To do so, we will have to confront those fears which the veil of heteropatriarchal machismo has hidden from our view. Foremost among these fears remains our culturally maintained fear of intimacy—of vulnerability and openness to another. This fear must become not an obstacle but a doorway instead—a doorway to self-transformation and self-healing; a doorway into the realization that our selves—our selfhood—will not dissipate in relationship; a doorway into mutuality and hence into intimacy and right relation. Acknowledging our fears may finally make intimacy and community possible.

Unfortunately, in our extremely sex-negative culture, our nakedness in sexuality, both literally and psychologically, provides an extremely powerful encounter with these fears of intimacy and loss of self. Before the onslaught of AIDS, the gay male subculture, far from liberating itself from this vicious dilemma posed by masculine socialization, instead institutionalized patterns of behavior which prevented both healthy confrontation with these fears and any possibility of intimacy. "Glory holes" which revealed not persons, but only penises, utterly blocked relational intimacy; darkened, music-filled bathhouses and orgy rooms likewise presented only vague bodily forms in fog and steam, while they precluded intimate communication and reduced the human participants again to merely genital machines; even the seemingly more personal one-night stands with bargoing "tricks" were generally begun under the veil of dim lights, loud music, and alcoholic haze, consummated often enough without so much as an exchange of names, and, when sobered by orgasm, were cleaned up and cleaned out of one's life as quickly as possible, lest the post-coital awkwardness give way—god/ess forbid—to any undesired intimacy. As we grow weary of these rituals and emerge from the long night of drugs, alcohol, and disembodied genitals to find ourselves growing older—and now after a decade of AIDS to also find ourselves surrounded by the fallen bodies of our comrades, those vast numbers of sexual acquaintances whom we never risked making our friends—we are stunned and shocked by this revelation. The second wave of our liberation will depend upon the survivors—not only upon those who survive AIDS, but also upon those survivors who are able to free themselves from the hetero-bracketed gaysexual underworld—survivors who must now wisely show us other ways to be sexual and to be sexual within the context of genuine intimate relation. Avoiding intimacy by means of a sexually driven promiscuity is the real threat to our selfhood—and to our lives—as gay men.

Recently Judith Plaskow has prophetically addressed our sexuality in a similar fashion. The goal of our liberation as gay people must not be merely a "blanket permission" for us to genitally act out our sexuality; rather, the goal of our liberation as gaysexual persons must be something more fundamental, more whole. A truly liberated sexuality is one which affirms the wholeness of our being as persons-in-relation: "Our sexuality is fundamentally about moving out beyond ourselves. The connecting, communicative nature of sexuality is not something we can experience or look for only in sexual encounters narrowly defined [as genital and/or anonymous], but in all real relationships in our lives."[18] Such utter self-affirmation accrues only without control, even though we find relinquishing control (i.e., vulnerability) frightening and difficult. We see sexuality as merely genital because we cannot handle a more thoroughgoing eros which permeates our lives, which breaks down our control, and which demands intimacy and relationship to create interpersonal wholeness. We have been taught, in short, that "eros is dangerous for a male."[19]

Reconceptualizing our sexuality, not as genital activities we accumulate separately from our ever-developing sense of self, but rather as the erotic energy which heals our lives, which enables us to be vulnerable and playful, and which seeks intimate friendship-in-mutual-relation, may altogether yet prove our salvation. Finally allowing the erotic to permeate our lives and to inform our relationships, while displacing the putative value of genital sexual acts, may enable us to achieve a vastly different and more fulfilling (wholistic) liberation than anything with which we have contented ourselves since Stonewall. Assertively claiming the power of eros permeating our body-selves, our lives, and our relationships—with intimacy, vulnerability, and playfulness—can enable us to reconceptualize, to reinvent, our sexuality in ways which shatter our self-punishing pasts with radical visions for the future, visions we must weave in the present. Both gender and sexual liberation theologies, for example, adamantly insist that body and soul, sexuality and spirituality are One; prophetically together we advocate the reconciliation of these but seemingly separate notions. We are one and we are our bodies.[20] Recently, for example, Judith Plaskow has echoed Nelson's concerns when she reiterates the extent to which our sexuality, our spirituality, and our need for relationship are all intertwined, interdependent, and one.[21] Not surprisingly, then, men's studies advocates and men's liberationists such as James Nelson have begun to realize that unity and cycles are far healthier concepts by which to understand our lives than dualisms and linearity. Particularly as we stand in the shadow of AIDS, which so vividly unites sexuality and death in our consciousness, Nelson goes on to insist that for men to recover and to reclaim both our bodiliness and a "sense of the cyclical"—the oneness of life, death, and renewal—is "to embrace less fearfully our finitude and mortality [and to] affirm not only the glories and pleasures of our embodiment but also their pains, not just our fleshly ecstasies but also the burdens and tragedies that our flesh can become."[22] In short, as fully integrated and unitary body-spirits, we will be more fully in touch with and engaged in all the multidimensional pluriformity of life-death as also a oneness and a oneness to celebrate even in the darkest moments which presage renewal.

Following through on these bold affirmations, Nelson then proceeds to ask a rhetorical question: "Is there not something good, important, and distinctive about the experience of maleness itself?"[23] He is, of course, convinced that this is so—that our bodiliness reveals something divinely intended for us.[24] As he works through both sexual essentialism and sexual constructionism, vis-a-vis men's bodies and our sexuality, his reflections reveal a more clearly theological bent. His quest is a search in men's bodily experience—specifically in the experiences of men's bodiliness, sexuality, and genitalia—for ways to transcend the unliberating images, confines, and socialization inherent in traditional Judaism and Christianity. In an effort, therefore, to (re)create a more liberating symbology for male embodiedness, he turns his attention specifically to our male genitalia and to the potentially deeper meanings of both erection and flaccidity. He is especially concerned to displace the overvaluation of performance-anxious, ever-ready erection with a reappreciation of the value of flaccidity, of being at rest.[25] He goes on to explain "phallus" (or erection) and "flaccidity" as symbolic metaphors of the masculine subconscious. The erect phallus represents strength, hardness, determination, penetration, and the vitality for life which manifests itself in both achievement and transcendence. The dark side, however, of the active and erect phallic male is manifest in sexual brutality and hierarchical oppression (over all things designated as "other"). In all its aspects, then, the erect phallus symbolizes "doing." In contrast, flaccidity represents "being," the "letting go of all urgency," which is not at all goal-directed.[26] Nelson argues that this represents our real experience the majority of the time; we are in fact more often flaccid than erect.[27] Championing a revaluation of flaccidity for masculine self-understandings, he ultimately implies that, when viewed not merely as phallic instruments, our male genitalia are actually cyclical, representing a constant alternation between life and death.[28]

He subsequently argues for a healthy reunion of being and doing for men, so that we may develop a more genuinely whole masculinity and masculine sexuality. We need both relationality in order to be aroused and gentleness in order to be strong. Evoking yet another part of our anatomy to underscore his conflation or reunion of apparent opposites, he adds, "Men [also] know the vulnerability of their testicles. ...Indeed, male vulnerability is most present exactly at the spot where colloquial language locates male courage"—in our balls![29] Moving from this image, his concluding thoughts on the symbology of male genitalia reemphasize the importance of integration and balance:

> To be fully masculine ... means embracing the fullness of the revelation that comes through our male bodies. There is good phallic energy in us which we can claim and celebrate. ...Equally important and equally male, there is good penile energy in us. It is soft, vulnerable, and receptive. It is a peaceful power. ...It is that strength of mutuality which can be enriched by other life without losing its own center.[30]

Nelson is clearly to be applauded for his daring work which contravenes millennia of heteromale, patriarchally masculine socialization. His painfully honest self-examination, reflections, and insights themselves embody the ballsy, vulnerable strength which he describes. Nevertheless, this otherwise healthy analysis and symbology is severely limited by its unwitting heterosexism: Although his goal is a unitary balance of erection and flaccidity—of phallic and penile energy—where "downtime" realistically predominates, he still begins with a dualism reminiscent of patriarchal hierarchies—phallic (erect) vs. penile (flaccid). Are his insights, therefore, genuinely reconciliatory and unifying, or does he not merely reverse the values assigned to these hierarchical polarities by championing receptive penile energy? Likewise, although his aim is the reconciliation of body and soul, sexuality and spirituality—an internalized integrity of the male— does not his focus on our external male genitalia subliminally sustain a masculine alienation or separation of ourselves from these external parts? What nongay man has ever truly and literally internalized male sexuality? Nelson is restricted, most unfortunately, to thinking only with his genitals.

In other words, if we are truly and radically going to claim that we are our bodies and that this oneness has spiritual and theological value as well as implications for our liberation as sexual beings, our work must be more thoroughgoing still. Our whole bodies are erotic; the erotic permeates our whole being. For gay men at least, whose experiences of embodied eroticism need not be limited to our genitals, the analysis (and celebration) of bodily experience must go beyond elucidating the metaphorical meanings of our external genitalia, to examine the mean-ings and implications of the full range of our erogenous zones as body-selves—to examine our whole erotic body. For example, gay men relish play with their nipples, their armpits, their asses. Oral experiences of sucking, biting, chomping, and swallowing evoke psychological and spiritual images of hungering and nurturing, of feeding and being fed. Likewise, the range of gay anal experience takes masculine receptivity far beyond simple nongay flaccidity; gay men are receptive to thrusting, to sometimes vast fullness, to direct prostate encounters which open us womblike to the world, both giving ourselves and receiving our partners. Gay men are also simply more open to erogenous/erotic bodily playfulness between good friends and spouses. Heteromale erotic embodiedness, especially between men themselves, is still very patriarchally restricted and confined.

Overall, then, the process of re-envisioning our sexuality begins with the adamant reaffirmation that our sexuality permeates all of who we are as persons and as gay men: Our sexuality should in no case be reduced to "merely genital functions." The erotic, or more concretely in our experience, our sexuality, becomes a meaningless, genitally-reduced notion unless we understand the erotic as part and parcel of our urges toward mutuality and human(e)ness. To be human is to be in relationship—with ourselves, with other persons, with the earth and the cosmos, and with god/ess. Our fundamental need for connectedness, love, and self-affirming acceptance— our erotic and sexual drive toward connectedness with all things—undergirds our quest for mutuality and, through the realization of that quest, for the establishment of justice in all relationships, not just our sexually expressed ones. And that is god/ess-with-us!

[1] Al Cotton, "Forward: On Gay Curmudgeons and Buccaneers," *Diary of a Southern Queen: An HIV+Vision Quest* (J. M. Clarck; Dallas, Monument Press, 1990), pp. v-viii.

[2] J. Michael Clarck, *Masculine Socialization and Gay Liberation: A Conversation on the Work of James Nelson and other Wise Friends* (with Bob McNeir; Dallas: Publishers Associates, under review [1992]).

[3] James B. Nelson, *Between Two Gardens: Male Sexuality and Religious Experience* (New York: Pilgrim Press, 1983), pp. 181-182.

[4] James B. Nelson, *The Intimate Connection: Male Sexuality, Masculine Spirituality* (Philadelphia: Westminster Press, 1988), p. 113.

[5] Ibid., pp. 38, 39.

[6] Ibid,. pp. 48 ff.

[7] J. Michael Clark, *A Defiant Celebration: Theological Ethics and Gay Sexuality* (Garland, TX: Tangeluld Press, 1990), pp. 113.

[8] Nelson, 1988, op cit., p. 40.

[9] Ibid., p. 40.

[10] Ibid., p. 12.

[11] Nelson, 1983, op cit., pp. 46-47.

[12] Nelson, 1988, op cit., p. 34.

[13] Ibid., pp. 34,35.

[14] Ibid., p. 37.

[15] Nelson, 1983, op cit., pp. 48,49.

[16] Nelson, 1988 op cit., p. 33.

[17] Ibid.

[18] Judith Plaskow, "Toward a New Theology of Sexuality," *Twice Blessed: On Being Lesbian, Gay and Jewish* (Eds., C. Balka & A. Rose; Boston: Beacon Press, 1989), pp. 145-146.

[19] Nelson, 1988, op cit., p. 55.

[20] Ronald E. Long, "God Through Gay Men's Eyes: Gay Theology in the Age of AIDS," *AIDS, God and Faith: Continuing the Dialouge on Constructing Gay Theology* (R. E. Long & J. M. Clarck; Dallas, Monument Press, 1992), p. 14.

[21] Plaskow, op cit., pp. 143-144.

[22] Nelson, 1988 op cit., pp. 82, 80.

[23] Ibid., p. 80.

[24] Ibid., p. 27.

[25] Ibid., p. 43.

[26] Ibid., p. 96.

[27] Ibid., p. 95.

[28] Ibid., p. 96.

[29] Ibid., p. 100.

[30] Ibid., p. 110.

IV. Craig W. Pilant

"We Shine a Ferocious Light": The Gay Community as Wounded Healers

> We pass level looks across the table, as things keep getting more and more dangerous. We strenuously reject not only the old stereotypes but the newer, well-intended oversimplifications. We try to tell ourselves and other people what we're learning from our anger and our loss and the upper reaches of our fear. We try to comfort one another. We shine a ferocious light.[1]

1. A Preliminary Observation

While observing patterns of inculturation of outsiders into the American mainstream, the historian, R. Laurence Moore, described the Americanization process in the following way: Despite what (historian) Frederick Jackson Turner wrote, most people who lived in this country did not gain a sense of what it meant to be an American by going to the (western) frontier. Far more of them gained that sense by turning aspects of a carefully nurtured sense of separate identity against a vaguely defined concept of mainstream or dominant culture.[2] Moore maintains that the defining element in the Americanization process was not the frontier in any of its manifestations. Unlike Turner's "frontier thesis" the fundamental self-defining element in the process of inculturation lay within the individual.

It is this paper's contention that a distinctive and unique contribution to American society can be made by gay men and lesbians—a contribution based on their unique individual and collective experiences. This contribution lies in the realm of becoming healers in a broken and wounded world. However, in order to discuss such a role, we must first ask whether we can make a contribution in light of the problematic inculturation of gay men and lesbian women—especially those who are white—into the American mainstream.

A great deal of verbiage has been written and spoken over the years, maintaining that gay men and women are fundamentally compatible to the mainstream of society. In the name of toleration, acceptance and civil rights, gays in America have followed the path that most "non-mainstream" groups (e.g., Catholics, Jews, southern Europeans) have pursued in the past. Religious and ethnic groups have sought integration into mainstream American society, to greater or lesser degrees of success. These attempts have been achieved by complex histories of group adaptation(s) and modifications in the values, norms, tolerances, concepts, and behaviors in the mainstream society itself.

For gay women and men, however, mainstreaming has appeared as both desireable and as an often-delayed dream. The attraction and desireability of inculturation is fairly obvious: the mainstream of the gay and lesbian population would facilitate relationship-building, community-bonding, goal attainment, as well as general psychological and physical well-being, not to mention safety. But this mainstreaming seems to be temporally a long-way off, especially when the spectre of homophobia, sexism and racism reveal their terrible realities among us.

This paper proposes that what the greater community of lesbian women and gay men needs to face is not the question of *when* inculturation into the American mainstream is to take place. Rather, I propose that the salient question is *whether* such an acclimatization should take place at all. Is such a mainstreaming truly and ultimately desireable for the greater good of the gay and lesbian population?

Does inculturation demand compromise and—to some extent—capitulation to the expectations of the already-dominant mainstream population?

It already appears that much of the history and experiences—social, sexual, interpersonal, etc—of gay women and men have diverged from those of heterosexuals. One might even ask whether new paradigms of interrelationship, bonding, sexual behaviors, and committment should develop in the future, especially in light of the AIDS epidemic. And if this is true, should not gay men and women be outside of mainstream pressures which would be exacerbated by mainstreaming?

I raise this question at the beginning of this paper for two reasons. First of all, if one considers this possibility then we can see the appropriateness of historian R. Laurence Moore's comment on the development of the peculiar way(s) in which outsiders become American. Here the uniqueness of being gay modulates the process of becoming American, just as it did (and still does) for ethnically diverse peoples who have come to these shores. By retaining one's individuality as a lesbian or gay man—and thereby remaining part of a people called "gay and/or lesbian"—one attains the quality of American-ness which, according to Moore, unites one to the greater society. In short, the more one remains an individual and an outsider, the more one becomes part of the society.

As with all ethnic and religious groups, however, the drift into the mainstream becomes at times irresistible. Little compromises are inevitable, and so often one finds oneself and one's group inculcated into the norms and values of the dominant society. Needless to say, a conscientious gay man or lesbian woman would probably bristle at the thought of embodying many of the racist, sexist or classist attitudes which have become part of this society.

This observation leads me to the second reason for this preliminary consideration of the question of mainstreaming the gay and lesbian population. As I will argue below, the gay and lesbian population faces a crisis of sorts. When the AIDS crisis becomes a matter of our history and our deeply imbedded memories, and when the major crises over civil rights and justice issues have been superceded by some form(s) of legal stabilty, I believe that the gay and lesbian community will face a period of self-defining. How is that self-defininition to be achieved unless there is the freedom to undertake it free of external pressures or the need to compromise?

Some years ago while reading some long-forgotten article, I came across a story about an Italian group of homosexuals who were working to achieve civil liberties and freedom from persecution in Italy. Though I do not remember the exact name of their organization, I do remember the acronym for the organization: *F.U.O.R.I.*, the Italian word for "outside."

As most if not all lesbians and gay men realize, "outsidership" is part of the identity of being homosexual. For decades, if not centuries, gay women and men have heeded the basic outsider philosophy: Avoid trouble and lie low, since visibility results in trouble. Gays, like African-Americans, Jews, and Catholics (among others), have experienced forms of harassment and persecution during certain periods of time in the English-speaking world. But unlike those other groups, mainstreaming or inculturation has generally only been done when suppressing all evidence of one's identity. African-Americans cannot suppress their skin color, and Jews and Catholics cannot easily hide their denominational and/or religious practices. Inculturation of lesbians and gays as lesbians and gays into the mainstream can only be done through conventional means of law and ordinance.

However will these means of inculturation lead to more subtle forms of suppression through compromise and/or capitulation? And if so, will lesbians and gays lose their unique presence within the dominant society? We can postulate that such an amalgamation into society possibly might also lose for the greater gay and lesbian community the opportunity for a unique collective role within the American society, a role which has already been demonstrated by many individual gay men and women.

To discuss such a role—that of the wounded healer—is the subject of the remainder of this paper. But we must remain cognizant that this role may be contingent upon the state of and the status of gays and lesbians within society.

2. *Gays and Lesbians as Wounded Healers*

In the opening chapter of her book, *America: Religion and Religions,* Catherine Albanese recounts the ancient Buddhist tale of the blind men who, upon coming upon an elephant, attempted to describe the creature.[3] From their various perspectives—determined by the part of the elephant which each man touched—the elephant was described variously as a long rope, a tree trunk, a great snake, an immense wall, and as a giant fan. Each simile was in part correct, yet each was also lacking the greater perspective due to their lack of vision. The proverbial tree was once again mistaken for the forest.

The past fifty years of the greater American public gay community—if we may be allowed to speak of a larger context for gays and lesbians in America—have had numerous brushes with that metaphorical elephant in the dark. From the cautious period of the Mattachine Society, through the heady days of Stonewall and the explosion of gay liberation in the seventies, up to and through the era of AIDS, the gay community at-large has been propelled from one experience to another in movements of self-discovery and exploration.

Just as a growing and developing person needs to discover itself in relation to the world and to encounter the world outside in reference to itself, so too has the gay community moved through the past several decades in search of mutuality. The vehicles for this voyage of discovery have been both multitudinous and varied: literature and pornography; music and dance; opera as well as disco; food and festivities; bars and bathhouses; politics as well as the Broadway stage; parades and protests; *The Advocate* "Interviews" and "Peek-a-boo" boxes; psychotherapy, sex and celibacy; controlled and not-so-controlled drugs; Axion, Dignity, Integrity, and (even) Courage: all of these and so many more have been means by which the multifaceted and multi-fractured gay community has attempted to move as an increasingly visible "body" through its puberty (the 1970's?), towards young adulthood as part of the larger culture.

And then there is AIDS, what many of us consider to be a watershed—if not the watershed—event in the history of the amorphous gay community. But what is beyond the AIDS crisis? And what is beyond the eventual attainment of acceptance and respect for the gay and lesbian communities? What role will (and do) gay and lesbian communities play in the larger human community? Beyond sexual and socio-political liberation, what is the purpose of this community?

It is the hypothesis of this paper that the painful and yet inspiringly hope-filled history of lesbians and gay men can assist us to serve humanity in a unique manner: as "wounded healers" for the human community. Using Henri Nouwen's concept of "the wounded healer," this paper will posit three models of how both gay/lesbian individuals and groups have and can assist the healing of humanity through socio-

political activism, through artistic creation and
through individual personalized ministry.

For the gay community, the AIDS crisis has
acted as both a magnifying lens as well as what the
great lesbian poet Elizabeth Bishop termed as "a
mirror upon which to dwell."4 More than any other
event, this crisis has brought the gay community and
its concerns into the consciousness of the American
public, causing our community to be under constant
scrutiny by observers—both sympathetic and
adversarial. For the gay community, however, the
AIDS crisis has acted as a mirror in which to behold
itself in its multiple manifestations and
incarnations—both philanthropic and self-centered.
The crisis—this "mirror upon which to dwell"—has
revealed depths previously only hinted at in our
literature, music and social activism.

AIDS entered not only our vocabularies and
newspapers, but also into the lives and bodies of
those we hold familiar and beloved. As the crisis
deepened, a radical change came over significant
segments of the gay community. First prophetic
(and even strident) voices arose—such as that of
Larry Kramer—who warned us not only of sorrow
and pain, but also of negligence and indifference
from the government, health industries and religious
sectors. Kramer's *The Normal Heart* 5 and William
Hoffman's *As Is* 6 were written in those early
harrowing days when hope seemed ephemeral and
religious oppression unrelenting.

As the epidemic settled in for the long haul, less
polemical and more reflective works appeared, such
as Paul Monette's *Borrowed Time.*6 Films—at first
infrequent and somewhat tentative—were released,
such as An Early Frost, providing admittedly
inadequate vehicles for expressions of fear of loss
and death in the gay community. Later films have
ranged from the truly mawkish (consider *Men in
Love*) to the restrained, yet moving *Longtime
Companion* and *André's Mother.*

But as literature, film and even dance came to terms with the developing stages of the AIDS crisis, rituals and music beg the question, what comes next? Unlike books and films, rituals and music tend to be open-ended, as if to cajole us into what comes after, or, better yet, into what comes as a result of what has been experienced. If one has ever been to an AIDS quilt display, or to a (now-politically incorrect) balloon release after an AIDS memorial service, one recognizes that the deceased individual will not be forgotten. The services also remind us that life continues to go on even after an event which commemorates the passing of a person who has died. People leave the site to go to a reception, or to work or to whatever obligations remain for the living. The living have their lives to continue, even after recognizing loss and bereavement.

Loss and bereavement not only fit into our lives as a moment in time, but also as an agent of change. One recent example of this is a work which the American (and openly gay) composer, John Corigliano wrote for the Chicago Symphony Orchestra in 1989. His *First Symphony* was written as a memorial for several friends who had died of AIDS. But for all of its harrowing power—best exemplified in the demonic Scherzo-Tarantella written to commemorate a friend who went insane just before his death due to toxoplasmosis- this work embodies the afterwards of loss and bereavement. This work, which can be heard in a recent recording, was written as a result of what had transpired.[7] How well Corigliano succeeds in his work is measurable in the metamorphosis of loss into creativity, the manifestation of change made perceptible.

Perceptible change has certainly been a hallmark of gay life since AIDS. The emergence of visible and vocal political and social action groups demonstrates the striking changes in the gay community. Not only have health care organizations, such as Body Positive and Gay Men's Health Crisis (GMHC), become visible and active, but groups such as ACT-UP and Queer Nation have taken on militant and (to some) offensive actions which cause upset, prompt rage, and even create alarm within many gay and straight communities. Designed to wake-up the complacent, these actions form symbolic and often effective catalysts for changes in attitudes and in the political landscape. Who knows where AZT and other experimental drug research might be today were it not for the overt political pressure placed by such groups on the FDA and CDC?

But what happens to all of this creativity, activism and generosity of spirit once the AIDS crisis is resolved? What happens as other socio-political battles are gradually resolved? Will gay men and lesbian women return to focus primarily on their own personal and/or community concerns, or are there other scenarios?

With all of the suffering, persecution and ostracism which the gay community has experienced in the past, I would posit that the collective history of gays and lesbians does allow for at least one other option besides that of self-concern. The Belgian-American writer, Henri Nouwen, has proposed a model for the individual person which—for all its idealism—can offer an alternative for members of the gay and lesbian community. This is the model of the "wounded healer."[8]

Nouwen originally proposed his model for the professional ministry. However, the image of the individual minister who suffers as being a person who is present as a healing source for others is a powerful and—to my mind—an irresistible one for this community. Evil, persecution and epidemic disease need to have meaning in order to transcend the pain, pathos and despair which remain in the wake of such suffering. The Judeo-Christian tradition is especially demanding in the transformation of the experience of evil into redemptive meaning, not only for the self but also for the larger community. The Jesus story, the parable of Job, and even the mythic story of the first man and woman, all have transformative aspects which go beyond the microcosm into the macrocosmos.

Nouwen postulates that the wounds of the individual—and, by extension, the wounded community—have power. As the wounded who would be healed, we as a wounded community have a source of consolation and healing for those others who are wounded. That consolation is to be found in our own lives and stories. In short, we can transform our woundedness into "a major source of healing power."[9] The wounds of the gay community are many—alienation, isolation, legalized second-class status, neglect, discrimination—and the sources of those wounds are many—government, church, societal institutions, traditions, mores, and laws. But the gay community can be healed of its woundedness by the creative life-affirming transformation of those wounds into an ethical life for others' healing. Through the process of healing members of the community can, in turn, become healers to other wounded members of the world community. (And these need not only be for members of the human family, but also extend to the realm of nature.)

I have chosen Nouwen's model as particularly appropriate to the gay community because of its connections to some all-too-familiar aspects of the gay experience. To Nouwen, the wounded healer is one who has experienced alienation, isolation and loneliness.[10] How much have those been intrinsic experiences to the lesbian woman or gay man in the search for companionship and community? From the lonely search for the other comes deepened appreciation of communion and shared lives. It is when the other opens the closed door to the individual in an expression of welcoming hospitality, that the wounded individual perceives that she or he is no longer alone, and that a graced existence involves others.

Hospitality, according to Nouwen, is "the virtue which allows us to break through the narrowness of our own fears and to open our houses to the stranger, with the intuition that salvation comes to us in the form of (the needful other), creating a free and fearless place for the unexpected visitor."[11] That hospitality need not be a place or even of a tangible nature. It may be of the spiritual, artistic or even political type, which expresses both a kind of hope-filled generosity of spirit as well as achievement. This generosity welcomes the wounded person into a universe of creativity and dynamic potential. At this point, we might point to the great generosity and love expressed by lesbian women in assisting their gay brothers during the AIDS epidemic—an act that bridged the separation which existed between the lesbian and gay communities. Their overwhelming response is a source of great encouragement and hope.

The wounded individual can find in his or her welcome inspiration not only to survive but also to be healed and to become productive and creative. By extension, the gay community can become capable or—to use an overused term—empowered to assist other troubled or needful communities.

A caution here. Not all peoples will want to accept the gift of healing. One wonders whether a person such as Kimberly Bergalis would be a willing recipient. But that is the nature of a gift—one may offer it, but the giver cannot and should not coerce the receiver into acceptance.

To illustrate briefly the possibilities inherent to the application of the wounded healer notion to the gay community, I have chosen four gay men who have demonstrated both the creativity and the healing potential of which I have just spoken. Each of these men utilized their struggles with their sexuality and transformed their isolation and pain into something creative and life-giving for others. The first example is taken from the international political stage, the second from the world of music, the third from the active religious ministry, and the last from the world of the stage. Each of these men have been selected since they represent various degrees of transforming personal pain and struggle into creative and life-affirming actions. These individuals also represent men whose own degree of being part of the larger society contrasts with their own visibility as gay men.[12]

Dag Hammarskjöld, the Swedish-born Secretary-General of the United Nations, who died in 1961, is an example of the wounded healer in the political realm. Though an intensely private man and one who left virtually public sexual history, Hammarskjöld left us a journal of remarkable self-revelation, entitled *Markings (Vägmärken)*. He termed it a "sort of white book concerning my negotiations with myself—and with God."[13] His lifetime spanned a fifty-five year period before Stonewall, and was lived in form of celibacy not so much as a denial of sexuality as, rather, a form of displacement of sexual fulfillment at the service of his people and of world peace. This wounded man reveals his dualistic nature in his poetry and prose:

> I came to a time and place where I realized that the Way leads to a triumph which is a catastrophe,and to a catastrophe which is a triumph, that the price for committing one's life would be reproach.[14]

But even knowing this about him does not diminish the example he gave as negotiator, politician, economic financier, and eventually Secretary-General. His death in the pursuit of peace in the then-war-torn Congo elevated him to the status of martyr in the eyes of the world community. And, despite attempts to deny or downplay the internal evidence given in his writings about the nature of his sexuality, Hammarskjöld can still be admired by us today. Though he presents a somewhat problematic figure for us in the post-liberation 1990's, we need to recognize that for a person living in the 1950's and early 1960's he managed to transform his self-perceived woundedness—and resulting virtual isolation—into a life of service and sacrifice for the benefit of humanity.

In the world of the arts, many admirable models of gay men and lesbian women have come down to us. However the late Leonard Bernstein provides us with a unique example of the transformation of an internationally-renowned composer and conductor (and much more!) into an exemplar of how to channel the creative drive into statement of eloquence, wit and compassion. Whoever among us who has had the good fortune to have heard his conducting know of Bernstein's moving love for music. But it is his own compositions that for a listener radiates a singular healing quality that is unique even in the world of Bernstein's music making. Any person who has heard the closing pages of either his *West Side Story* or *Candide,* or the "Agathon" movement of the *Serenade for Violin, String Orchestra and Percussion,* let alone the troubled resolutions of urban schizophrenia and alienation in his opera, *A Quiet Place,* or in the *Kaddish* and *The Age of Anxiety* symphonies, cannot be but overwhelmed at the love for humanity which Bernstein manifests in these works. This healing power was due not just to his compositional prowess, but also to who this conflicted man was as manifested in his journey of self-discovery in music towards personal healing and resolution.[15]

Michael Peterson, who died of AIDS at the age of 44, is perhaps a name who is unknown to most people outside of his home in Washington, D.C. However, in the Archdiocese of Washington, and among AIDS workers and activists, he was a singular example of compassion and decency. Peterson was the founder of the St. Luke Institute for clergy and religious men and women who were suffering from chemical, alcoholic and sexual disorders. A tireless advocate dealing compassionately with displaced workers, the homeless, and the severely ill in his capacity as psychiatrist, physician, and priest, Peterson spent his last several years as a Person-with-AIDS as both activist and minister. His active years were lived as a witness to the verities of his own life, and as a healer of and for those around him. Out of the struggles and pain of his own life, he brought light and inspiration amid the encircling gloom brought on by the AIDS epidemic.[16]

The last of the four persons I wish to describe is fortunately still very much with us and who is as active and productive as ever. Harvey Fierstein can easily be called a healer due to his writings and plays which emanate from his experience as a gay man. As a playwright, he has sought to use his own life experiences as a mirror of those of others in the larger gay community. Fierstein's wit and wisdom underline the need for honesty in relationships and the need for reality as well:

ARNOLD: I don't need anyone. Thank you.
ED: Well, maybe I do.
ARNOLD: Then go home. You've got a lovely wife who'd do anything for you. She can give you a home, a two-car garage, a child of your own, white

> picket fence... the whole shebang,
> double-dipped in chocolate and
> government-approved. Go home,
> Ed, I ain't got nothin' like that here.[17]

The need for independence and stabilty are carefully
explored in Fierstein's work. His personal struggles
with actualizing himself in light of his sexuality have
enabled him to transform his pain into a realistic
landscape of what it means to be gay in America.

But his message is not one of bitterness. Rather
it is a demand for the right to be acknowledged as a
full human being. In a protracted argument with his
Jewish mother. Fierstein's alter ego, Arnold Becker,
proclaims his fundamental creed for relating to the
rest of the world and, especially, to his mother:

ARNOLD: There's one more thing you've got to
            understand....   Let me tell you
            something; I have taught myself to
            sew, cook, fix plumbing, do taxes,
            build furniture... I can even pat
            myself on the back when necessary.
            All so I don't have to ask anyone for
            anything. There is nothing I need
            from anyone except love and respect.
            And anyone who can't give me those
            two things has no place in my life.[18]

Though his creed is somewhat reductionistic, how
many other gay men and lesbian women have found
themselves in similar situations when the pressure on
them to compromise themselves has brought them to
some form of ultimatum with those they love?
Fierstein demonstrates the need for both love and
dignity in one clear utterance. He also expresses the
need for risk as well, clearly demarcating the limits
of love and human intercourse with family and
friends should they fail to affirm his personhood and
self-esteem. By revealing his own pain and

suffering—as well as joy and ultimate hope—
Fierstein allows the public to view his private world
through the stageworks he creates and the alter egos
he embodies with his own philosophy of life. He
gives his life deeper meaning by opening his psychic
wounds for the good of others through the works he
writes for the theatre.

Harvey Fierstein's own life story, as well as
those of Michael Peterson, Dag Hammarskjöld, and
Leonard Bernstein, all embody the realization that the
life of an individual must have a purpose in order to
give some meaning not just to one's own being, but
also to one's existence in a larger context. Whether
that context is the gay community or the larger
world, the transformation called for in the individual
is akin to what is termed "metanoia". In order to
attain purpose, one must undergo a change of heart,
a "turning-around," a conversion of sorts. Here we
are not talking so much of a religious conversion—
though this could provide the fertile ground for what
we are inferring—as well as for further discourse.
Rather, we are rather perceiving a change which
turns us outwards towards and for others, especially
other suffering peoples. Hammarskjöld's concern
for the Third World which led to his tragic death,
Bernstein's compassion for the alienated and
disenfranchised through his musical and political
activities, Peterson's empathetic response to the
physically, psychologically and spiritually ill,
Fierstein's witty and sagacious world-view of what it
means to be human for the benefit of the theatre-goer:
all of these models are examples of who and what the
gay community in its individual parts and in its
totality can be for the rest of the human family.

Shouldn't this be true for all human beings? Of
course. However, gay men and lesbian women—
because of their unique history of suffering,
persecution, and alienation—have a special role in
the world. To be healers for a broken world is not
merely some idealistic concept. Who better can

understand the persecuted than those who experienced it themselves? Who can better assuage the tears of the suffering than those who have endured pain? Who can reconcile the alienated better than those who have been shunned and ostracized by their own families and friends? To minister as wounded healers is the natural destiny of the gay community, stemming from a uniquely-singular collective and individual experience as part of the human family.

[1] Michael Cunningham, "After AIDS, Gay Art Aims for a New Reality." *The New York Times,* April 26, 1992, 2. 1, V.

[2] R. Laurence Moore, *Religious Outsiders and the Making of Americans* (New York: Oxford University Press, 1986), p. xi.

[3] Catherine Albanese, *America: Religions and Religion* (Belmont, CA: Wadsworth Publishing Company, 1981), p. 1.

[4] Elizabeth Bishop, "Insomnia," in *Poems: North & South - A Cold Spring* (Boston: Houghton Mifflin Company, 1940), p. 76.

[5] Larry Kramer, *The Normal Heart* (New York: New American Library, 1985).

[6] Paul Monette, *Borrowed Time: An AIDS Memoir* (New York: Avon Books,1988).

[7] Recorded by Daniel Barenboim and the Chicago Symphony Orchestra at the world première performances, March 15-17, 1990, in Orchestra Hall, Chicago, and released on Erato Compact Disc, No. 2292-45601-2.

[8] Henri J.M. Nouwen, *The Wounded Healer: Ministry in Contemporary Society* (New York: Doubleday, 1972). Nouwen uses the term "wounded" to refer here to the idea of injury, not debilitation. Woundedness in religious parlance so often refers to notions of incapacitation, passivity and resigned acceptance. Here we intend to jettison the notion of this romanticized notion and view the term in all of its Anglo-Saxon bluntness: a wound incurs pain and injury, but not defeatism. As *Webster's New Lexicon Dictionary* states, it also infers a "mark" or "scar". Such a mark or scar gives evidence by which the once-inflicted wound is known and acknowledged, but is, in the course of time, healed and made whole.

[9] Ibid., pp. 82-3.

[10] Ibid., pp. 88-9.

[11] Ibid., p. 89.

[12] I personally regret the absence of examples of lesbian women from my list, though I believe that Eleanor Roosevelt would be one excellent example to include. However, linking her life's work with her struggles over sexuality are not readily documentable, despite recent biographical excursus to the contrary. Also, it seems that the aforementioned poet, Elizabeth Bishop, would also be a powerful example of a wounded healer. Unfortunately, I was unable to ascertain the certainty of this postulate in time for this paper's submission.

[13] Dag Hammarskjöld, *Markings (Vägmärken)* (New York: Alfred A. Knopf, Inc., 1964), p. v.

[14] Ibid., p. 180.

[15] And, needless to say, Bernstein's compassion was also manifested in his non-musical life as a sponsor and spokesperson for the suffering and dispossessed through his political and social advocacy work which was in itself remarkable in its range and persistence.

[16] *National Catholic Reporter* , v. 23, no. 26 (April 24, 1987), p. 5; *Origins* , v. 16, no. 46 (April 30, 1987), p. 1ff.

[17] Harvey Fierstein, *Torch Song Trilogy* (New York: Signet Books, 1988), p. 178.

[18] Ibid., p. 163.

V. Michael L. Stemmeler

The Testing Game:
HIV-Antibody Testing as Exercise
of Socio-political Power

1. Introduction

Since the development of HIV-Antibody tests in the mid-1980s there have been calls for large scale testing of significant population groups. Often these calls were not raised order to get exact statistical information about the status of the AIDS health crisis or to be able to make accurate prognoses with regard to the medical, human, and economic cost of the epidemic. Rather these calls were levied in order to generate ideological support for the implementation of restrictive social policies. Politics had entered the AIDS health crisis.

About eleven million people worldwide have been infected with HIV and the majority of them are heterosexual. In the United States, however, the majority of those infected with the HIV are gay/bi-sexual men and gay/bi-sexual IV-drug users, followed by IV-drug users and women of color. These groups belong to socially ostracized and marginalized population groups. Neither gay men nor IV-drug users, nor the poor, ethnic minority woman is well liked by mainstream society. For whatever reason, the members of these groups are often perceived to be threats to the moral, social, physical and, medical well-being of society of which the power *élites* understand themselves as the true and only standard bearers. Members of these groups are also often categorized as "social ballast existences," to apply a loaded social-darwinist term from the 1920s.

Gays, for example, undermine the value system of society by privately and publicly challenging the established systems of moral behavior by using sexuality in an unorthodox and unlicensed way, thereby questioning radically the validity and the rationales of the sexual mores of the dominant society. IV-drug users also do not play by the rules of dominant society. They are disappointed about what society may be able to offer to them; they do not find their spot in the fabric of a society. They do not buy into the white male, middle-class rationale for what it means to be a good citizen who does not challenge the existing power structure. They do not think that they should be forced to support this structure through quiet submission.

The minority woman is not accepted by the establishment exactly because she is a member of a minority group. But she is also rejected because she is a woman who, because of her gender, has no place in the lines of power and therefore should not have any access to the benefits which the dominant society provides to its supportive members.

The privacy rights of the population groups just described are often not respected by the political establishment. The establishment only recognizes the rights of its "acceptable" members. In a variation of the "social contract" theory, the benefits of the social entity can only be enjoyed if one is already a member of the class that has established the benefits particularly for its own constituency. Whoever dares to differ for reasons of sexual orientation, skin color, private behavior, or economic condition is labeled an outsider from whom the members of the dominant class not only separate physically, but whom they also intend to control in order to avoid any radical challenge to their own existence.

By what means does the dominant society, through its medical, political, and business establishments, attempt to implement policies that control whatever is different or deemed threatening to the existing social and political order? It can be said at the outset that the medical and political establishments, unfortunately, have scored some successes in several areas.

The Centers for Disease Control have issued guidelines for the as of yet voluntary testing of health care providers. Several states have issued guidelines to the same effect and the U.S. Congress is debating the mandatory testing of all health care providers. The socio-political rationale for the existing guidelines is to protect society at-large from infection with HIV. From a community ethics point of view this may be laudable, were it not for the fact that only a miniscule percentage of health care seekers has actually been infected with HIV by an HIV-positive health-care provider or by someone in the health profession who has AIDS but chose to continue to work until the syndrome would make such activity impossible. The socio-political rationale far outdistances the expected benefits of such testing to society.

Most health care providers, doctors, nurses, laboratory assistants, etc., do not belong *qua* profession to the class of people whom the medical and political establishments intend to control. However, among the large class of health care providers are numerous people who for one reason or another fall into the above mentioned population groups which power *élites* may intend to control for their apparently unorthodox behavior in their private lives, such as gay people or IV-drug users. This seems reason enough for the political authorities to request screening of those groups in order to extrapolate anyone who may have challenged the norms and morals of society in some way outside of his/her professional environment.

How are HIV-testing policies used and abused as means of socio-political power? How do such policies, among other things, identify people with socially stigmatized behavior patterns and provide rationales for the control, and possibly exclusion, of such identified groups from the social process? Gay men are particularly at risk of being negatively affected by testing policies of whatever sort. For the most part they do not enjoy any privacy protection and they are not covered by most anti-discrimination laws. If these policies require *mandatory* screening for the presence of antibodies to HIV the risk to their social well-being is potentiated. Here it does not matter whether the testing policy specifies the clientele as health-care providers, health care seekers, or whether the testing goes on in business and industry in order to eliminate HIV-positive workers from company rolls. Gay men, an already marginalized population group, have to become conscious of the various forms of attacks against their beings and their lives from various sides under the guise of concern for the social and medical well-being of the entire population of which they are sometimes deemed to be an expendable part.

2. Requests for Large Scale HIV-Antibody Testing

a. From the Medical Community

Since HIV was identified as HTLV-III in 1983 as the most likely responsible agent for AIDS, calls for voluntary or mandatory testing have been raised by various voices within the medical community. One commonly heard argument expressed the necessity for large scale testing in the service of assembling purely epidemiological data about AIDS. Without a significantly sized pool of data about HIV infection of the entire population, it would be impossible to make any prediction with regard to the future impact of AIDS on society as a whole. Without an adequate data pool it would also be impossible to convince the political community that significant financial resources should be made available for research on HIV itself, particularly toward finding a cure for AIDS, a vaccine against HIV, or the development of treatment plans to alleviate the devastating effects of AIDS with regard to pain, suffering, and death of large population groups.

The medical community proffered medico-scientific rationales for its demands and compared HIV-Antibody testing to earlier large scale testing for epilepsy, diabetes, syphilis, and tuberculosis. No comparisons were drawn, however, to large scale sickle-cell anemia screening of African-American population groups in the past. That effort toward generating a medico-statistical data pool resulted in significant instances of discrimination against African Americans with and without the genetic irregularity. This type of medically rationalized discrimination potentiated the invidious discrimination already experienced by the African American community.

Often the reasons for requesting large scale antibody testing or screening were not informed by an ethically commendable concern for human welfare or the advance of medical knowledge in the fight against a deadly attacker. The reason for requesting large scale HIV-Antibody screening may have been the expectation that such screening would provide a convenient rationale for absolving oneself or the entire medical community from the duty to treat or to take care in any other way of people who were infected with the AIDS virus. This rationale for screening large population groups was rarely expressed publicly because of the possible embarrassment it could carry for the proponent of such a position.

Whether a hospital, a physician, or any other health care provider would make gained medical knowledge available in the service of health restoration or maintenance could possibly be tied to the results of such testing. Of course, large scale population testing does not of itself yet say anything about the serostatus of an individual human being who might seek the caretaking attention of a health care provider. It is, however, a qualitative difference only between conducting large scale screening programs on the one hand and identifying the serostatus of an individual who participated in such a screening program to health care providers, insurance companies, and to the participant her/himself.

Infection with HIV has become so common in some parts of the United States that hospitals are now experimenting with programs that implement some kind of routine screening of all their patients, which would include ambulant health care seekers. The Centers for Disease Control issued the call for precautionary screening of all patients. Only in that way would it be possible to respond professionally to the presence of HIV among the hospital population.

A CDC survey of 26 hospitals in 21 cities found that the rate of HIV for the general U.S. population was 0.4%, which translates into 1 million people. This is the number of people commonly quoted as being HIV infected.[1] Because the CDC survey was conducted in cities and not in rural areas of the U.S., the average rate of infection for the general population was 1.3%, which would translate into 3.25 million people, a rate significantly higher than the assumed 1 million HIV infected people nationwide. There was also a significant difference between the infection rate in cities of the western U.S. and in eastern regions. The cities in the western U.S. were small compared to the cities of the East Coast which were surveyed. The East Coast cities' rate of HIV infection was significantly higher.

In a study published in the *JAMA* (1990) Charles E. Lewis and Kathleen Montgomery investigated already existing HIV-testing policies of U.S. hospitals. Lewis and Montgomery surveyed a stratified random sample of all non-federal acute care hospitals. For this they used the American Hospital Association's 1987 database. The method of the survey was to conduct interviews with chief administrators with regard to the testing policy of a particular institution. The response rate reported was 78.4%. Of the 561 hospitals surveyed 66.6% had admitted at least one person with AIDS. 466 hospitals had some sort of written policy about HIV testing. Most of the policies had a provision for patients' rights, like pretest informed consent (78%). 66% of the hospitals had developed a special HIV-testing consent form. It is important to notice that 75% of hospitals surveyed required that any seropositive test would have to be related to the testee. The study does not mention whether any kind of pretest counseling took place at any location or whether those who tested HIV-positive received post-test counseling when they were informed about their serostatus. The latter type of counseling is regarded as particularly important in the discussion of ethically responsible testing activities.

What is interesting is the course of action the hospitals surveyed follow after they have received the test results. Entering a positive HIV test result into a patient's chart is cited as the rationale for the protection of health care providers. 56% of the hospitals require that the test result be entered into a patient's records. If a patient tests positive to the presence of antibodies to HIV, a revision of a specific treatment plan will take place which takes the positive serostatus of the patient into consideration. 17 of the hospitals surveyed require a transfer of the seropositive individual to another health care facility. Upon interrogation as to why such a policy was put into practice, two reasons were given. The first was the staff's fear of contagion and the second was the possible high cost of caring for HIV-infected patients. The possibility that another health care facility might be better equipped to care for an HIV-infected person was not ventilated.[2]

At this point it becomes evident that testing policies may have negative effects on the availability of health care for particular population groups. Given the fact that about 70% of HIV infected people and people living with AIDS are gay men, it becomes evident that access to adequate health care may be barred to an increasing number of people, if more hospitals should choose to implement more restrictive policies with regard to admitting HIV-positive individuals for care or should initiate the termination of such care at the time when the serostatus of an individual becomes known.

The high economic cost of caring for HIV infected individuals once they have developed the syndrome is influential in a hospital's decision to admit anyone who has tested positive. Many AIDS patients have only Medicare coverage, which often does not provide adequate reimbursement to the hospital.[3] The development of discrimination against HIV-Antibody-positive individuals and people with AIDS on economic grounds thus becomes evident.

Medically rationalized testing policies have
significant socio-political controlling effects. The
health-care provider only accepts people for treatment
who do not belong to a group of citizens who have to
rely on government assistance for the payment of
their health care bills.

The actual target of a hospital's policy to deny
access to health care to people on public payroll may
ideally be interpreted as a critique of the
government's inappropriate funding of the welfare
concerns of its citizens. What, in fact, happens is the
deliberate exclusion of impoverished people from the
health care system. It is public knowledge that you
have to become impoverished first in order to avail
yourself of government health care dollars. This hits
people who live with AIDS particularly hard. First
they have to exhaust all their available private
insurance moneys, if there are any, before federal,
state, or local social service systems kick in. But
then, exactly at the time when financial assistance is
needed the most to insure continued access to health
care, a log is thrown into the way of health care
accessibility by health care providers who refuse to
operate on the level of government social service
spending.

The other reason quoted by Lewis and
Montgomery for a hospital's implementation of a
testing policy was the staff's fears of contagion,
particularly by the nursing and surgical staff. It is
not surprising that the fears of the hospital personnel
were generally higher in hospitals *without* AIDS
patient experience.[4] Obviously a lot of education
needs to be done to bring nursing and surgical staff
up-to-date on virus transmission avenues, absence of
casual contact risks, and universal precautions in the
medical field.

Hospitals may also call for large scale HIV-
Antibody testing in order to support the "good"
reputation of the facility. Too many HIV-positive
patients admitted, or having to care for too many

people with AIDS, may be perceived as a stain on a hospital's "white gown" and result in a silent boycott of the facility by health care seekers, if they have the option to choose into which facility they want to be admitted and if they enjoy the financial wherewithal to follow up on their choice. If a hospital's testing policy and subsequent exclusion of positive testees is based on this rationale, it is catering to already existing detrimental stereotypes about easy contamination of the entire hospital environment with HIV and fears about the virus' transmission route via casual contact. Testing or screening policies in this case are the result of social pressures which have their roots in discriminatory stereotypes that marginalize or exclude those population groups which do not fit the accepted social mold. Underlying this frame of mind is the myth that orthodox, socially sanctioned behavior does not result in HIV-infection. Whoever has become infected has therefore made the decision to leave the social canon of behavior behind. This action merits the experience of punishment, *i.e.,* exclusion from the social sphere which manifests itself in one way by barring the infected person from access to health care.

If this is applied to gay men it becomes immediately evident why they suffer particularly from large scale testing policies. Their personal and sexual behavior is still regarded as situated largely outside the canon of socially accepted and acceptable behavior. It is therefore only right, so the rationalization goes, that they experience the punishment of becoming excluded from a health care system that is charged with taking care first of the "good" members of society, those who abide by social and sexual mores of the community.

b. *Calls From Politicians:*

Calls for large scale HIV-Antibody testing have also been raised by the political community. Herethe conservative/reactionary factions in federal, state, and local legislatures most frequently issue these calls. Often misinformed about the state of medical knowledge of the actual transmission routes of the virus and sometimes inspired by religiously fueled bigotry, certain politicians would like to test everyone who does anything in which society is in one way or another involved. Their agenda is to develop mandatory testing policies that cover every area of contact of an individual with society. Areas that have been identified so far are health care, prisons, job applicants for all types of jobs where an employee has contact with the public, food handlers, employment in health and beauty fields, and immigrants. This list is not conclusive and new areas will probably be identified soon. All branches of the military, for example, have had mandatory testing and screening policies in place for a number of years.

Particularly Senator Jesse Helms (R-N.C.) is on the forefront of requesting the expansion of mandatory testing to and test result reporting of all kinds of professional employees. Several days before the Centers for Disease Control issued their "Recommendations for Preventing Transmission of Human Immunodeficiency Virus and Hepatitis B Virus to Patients During Exposure-Prone Invasive Procedures,"[5] Helms presented the U.S. Senate with an amendment to a federal appropriations bill that makes it a federal crime for a doctor, a dentist or other health care professional who has AIDS and who knows it to perform invasive medical procedures without informing the patient. Violators of this bill could be fined $10,000, or could be imprisoned for not less than 10 years, or both.[6] As a rationale for his amendment Helms used the case of the late Kimberly Bergalis of Fort Pierce, FL, who was infected with HIV by her dentist who had AIDS and who continued to work and perform invasive dental procedures without informing his clients about his medical condition.

Helms plays on the fears of the public which he thinks has a right to know about the medical status of its health care providers with regards to HIV-infection and AIDS in order to make an informed choice, regardless of whether any contact between health care worker and patient would carry a risk. The fact that some health care providers may have infected their patients in the course of performing their professional activities is cited as sufficient reason to require all health care workers to subject themselves to periodical HIV-Antibody tests in order to satisfy the public's desire to know its health care providers' medical condition.

People like Jesse Helms exploit the fears of a largely un- or misinformed American public that holds mandatory testing to be the panacea for the entire AIDS health care crisis, as if the medical community could arrest the spread of the virus by simply having everybody tested. In his congressional pitch for the passing of the above mentioned amendment Helms quoted a June 1990 Gallup poll that found that 95% of the American people believed that surgeons should be required to tell patients if they are infected with the AIDS virus and that 94% believe that all physicians and dentists should be required to tell their patients that they have AIDS.[7]

Of course, it is a great tragedy on the personal level if even one human being is infected by a physician or any other health care provider with the AIDS virus. In the case of the Florida dentist it has been established that he treated about 1,700 people after he found out that he had AIDS. Some of those patients may also have become infected. What is known and established medical fact, however, is that a mandatory testing policy for health care providers does not do anything about the spread of the virus and about the syndrome itself. It does not do anything to limit transmission routes, and it certainly does not say anything about a health care provider's serostatus at the time when a patient turns to her/him with a treatment request. By the time treatment is provided a formerly seronegative person could have turned seropositive which is not known to that person until the time of the next test several months later. It also does not account for the fact that a person who has repeatedly tested negative for the presence of HIV-Antibodies may in fact be infectious and may have transmitted the virus to someone else in the exercise of her/his profession. Medical research has found that the HI-virus may be entirely inactive for several years, during which time not even antibodies may be formed.[8] Nevertheless, such an infected person without detectable antibodies may become the source of infection of someone else, if during an invasive procedure blood is accidentally exchanged.

Helms' amendment does not addresses this situation. In addition, it also commits the fallacy of identifying gaining first knowledge of one's positive HIV status with having AIDS, when, in fact, these are too entirely separate issues. Provided an individual is tested and the result is positive it may be well up to 10 years until this person may develop AIDS. Progress in the development of pharmaceuticals and other treatment options may delay the onset of AIDS even further in the future. Helms' amendment has no medical or social benefits. It is political in character, fueling public hysteria about AIDS related issues. It may, in fact, result in significant human and economic hardships to a health care provider whose patients depart because of mandatory serostatus disclosure, regardless of whether in the therapeutic course any exposure-prone invasive procedures would be performed.

The same is true for requests to test those who seek health care. A prior test for the presence of antibodies to HIV in the blood of an individual does not give any guarantee about the serostatus of an individual at the time that s/he is seeking health care. An on the spot test also would not reveal the serostatus positively since seroconversion may not yet have taken place. Universal precautionary procedures have to be employed in all cases as the best protection. That is exactly the code most physicians and hospitals have adopted as routine in the treatment of all health care seekers. The treatment of any human being as potentially infected with HIV and the application of appropriate protection measurements is the only effective way of preventing infection of either care provider or care seeker.

Calls from politicians for stringent mandatory testing policies may only backfire. Professional restrictions mandated for the HIV-positive physician can have the negative result of driving that health care provider out of his profession, thereby reducing the number of health care providers who are available for the needs of the general public and particularly for the needs of already HIV-infected people. Many HIV-positive health care providers have dedicated much of their professional attention to their HIV-positive and AIDS clientele. The *Michigan Recommendations on HIV-Infected Health Care Workers* [9] affirm that "[m]any infected as well as non-infected HCWs *[Health Care Workers]* have dedicated their professional services, at least in part, to the care of HIV-infected patients. Practice restrictions imposed on these HCWs would severely limit access to care by those most in need."

Political calls for mandatory testing, periodic screening, and serostatus revelation in certain professional environments are judgmental. They are based on particular moral perceptions and cater to the irrational fears of uninformed population groups. They may also serve to enlist the support of special interest groups and may turn out to be entirely punitive in nature.

3. What the Recommendations for Health Care Professionals actually say.

The Centers for Disease Control in Atlanta published their guidelines aimed at the prevention of transmission of HIV and Hepatitis B virus [HBV] in July of 1991.[10] Several states followed with the establishment of their own guidelines for health care workers, particularly those who were HIV-infected or who had already developed AIDS. As one state example the *Michigan Recommendations on HIV-Infected Health Care Workers* may be introduced.[11]

Both guidelines deal particularly with the health care provider and the responsibilities that may arise for the provider in case s/he has become infected with HIV or runs the risk of becoming infected in the line of work. The guidelines do not address the issues of testing the health care seeking clientele.

Right at the beginning of the CDC *Recommendations* it is unambiguously clear that even an HIV infected health care workers do not pose a virus transmission risk to anyone as long as they refrain from performing invasive procedures.[12] This clear affirmation of the absence of significant or even low risk to a patient in the care of such providers may serve as an argument against politically motivated calls for indiscriminate testing or periodical mandatory screening of health care providers.

HBV infected HCWs who adhere to universal precautions and who perform, certain exposure-prone procedures pose only an small risk for transmitting the hepatitis B virus. Since the transmission of HIV is considered to be more difficult than the transmission of HBV, it may be concluded that certain exposure-prone procedures can be performed by such infected persons since the risk for transmission of the virus to the patients is even less than the risk of transmission of HBV which already was deemed quite small.[13] The CDC conclude that "currently available data provide no basis for recommendations to restrict the practice of HCWs infected with HIV or HBV who perform invasive procedures not identified as exposure-prone, provided the infected HCWs practice recommended surgical or dental technique and comply with universal precautions and current recommendations for sterilization/disinfection."[14]

Nevertheless, the CDC also recommend that HCWs should be knowledgeable about their HIV-Antibody status and that in case they are positive they should not perform exposure-prone procedures unless they have sought counsel from a review panel of experts and have been advised under what circumstances they may continue to perform these procedures.[15] One such circumstance is the notification of prospective patients about the seropositive status of the health care provider and the permission of the client to go ahead anyway with the performance of an exposure-prone and/or invasive procedure.[16] It is this provision in the *Recommendations* which Helms addressed proleptically by legally mandating the disclosure of a health care provider's serostatus.

The federal as well as the Michigan State guidelines stay far away from recommending any large scale screening of health care providers, nor do they recommend mandatory testing for applicants in the health care field or mandatory periodic testing of HCWs. All they do is recommend that HCWs who perform certain exposure-prone and/or invasive procedures decide for themselves to become informed about their serostatus. Depending on the results of such voluntary tests, which may be obtained anonymously and confidentially, the HCW may choose to refrain from any activity that could pose a significant risk to a client.

Several months before the CDC issued its guidelines, the American Medical Association, the American Dental Association and other medical organizations went publicly on record as opposing any attempt toward mandatory testing of doctors. All groups said that such mandatory testing would not be necessary and would, in fact, be counterproductive. Mandatory testing would not protect patients from the slight possibility of contracting the AIDS-virus from infected health care personnel.[17] In addition, a restrictive interpretation of mandatory testing of health care providers could lead to a federally mandated job prohibition for HIV-infected HCWs. Testing policies with punitive effects were rejected by all medical associations as ethically unacceptable, socially counterproductive, and medically without benefit.

On the other hand, both the American Medical and the American Dental Associations support a policy that requires HIV-infected HCWs and those HCWs with AIDS to disclose their status to their patients. Invasive procedures could only be performed after a patient's consent had been obtained.[18] What are the ethical implications of being forced to disclose one's HIV-Antibody status? At the least it may mean the loss of a job. It can also result, however, in significant trauma to the health care worker's psycho-social, emotional, and economic well-being. Following appropriate precautions in the line of work, on the other hand, could render disclosure a moot point.

Literature and news features about the pros and cons of physician and other health care provider testing abounds. Frequently however, a central question is overlooked. What may be the social fallout of recommended testing for health care workers? Is there a socio-political agenda hidden also in proposals for voluntary *vs.* mandatory testing? Is mandatory testing of employees in certain job categories the next step? Are proposals for screening large population segments or the entire population already in the works?

4. What May Follow in the Shadow of Medical Guidelines.

The fallout from recommendations for HIV-Antibody testing from professional medical communities may be used as a jumping board for the development of mandatory testing policies in many areas of professional and social life. The "slippery slope" argument may be adducted to highlight the possible effects of federal and state guidelines for health care workers.

Common social and political wisdom regard many of the words coming from the mouth(s) of the medical community as gospel. If the medical community issues an opinion on a certain type of disease or on a treatment procedure, this opinion is highly respected by almost everyone. In the context of AIDS and HIV-infection this is particularly the case. Unfortunately, not everything the medical community has to say about HIV-infection and AIDS is adequately understood by the public or by politicians. Politicians see it as their goal to form public policies on the basis of the expert information they receive. Because much about HIV and AIDS is misunderstood to begin with, politicians have a tendency to react inappropriately. This often takes the form of overreaction. In addition to their own misunderstanding about the issues involved, politicians also try to placate those segments of the public that keep them in power.

Misunderstandings and public fears about HIV and AIDS have led to a climate in which the political community is trying and failing to manage a health crisis entirely with political means, one of which is the social control of the population by making HIV tests mandatory or advocate mass screenings. The danger of the medical guidelines does not lie so much in the fact that they recommend testing for certain medico-professional groups but in the fact that they are abused by political and industrial power *élites* to request the development of strict testing policies, which in the most far reaching case would cover the entire population. The rationale for this kind of request lies in the belief that if the medical community recommends testing for certain employee groups, it may also be beneficial for the social welfare if large population groups are tested, preferably those about whose social standing one has significant doubts. These groups are also the easiest targets because they do not always have vocal legal advocacy groups that may fight for their rights.

The argument goes that if the medical community recommends testing its people one might as well go a step further and require first the testing of medical employees, but then expand this policy of mandatory testing to other social environments. In certain areas such requests have already gained a foothold, without generating much success one may add. But then the question is immediately, what is defined as success? If screening is performed for any other reason than collecting epidemiological data is is very hard to construct success. In addition, for the collection of epidemiological data all screening could be done with testee consent in anonymous and confidential environments.

Mandatory screening programs in the U.S. have not been anonymous and opinions diverge with respect to confidentiality. Known programs include premarital screening for HIV-Antibodies in Illinois and Louisiana, testing of applicants for service in all branches of the armed forces, screening of all service personnel already in the military, mandatory testing for all immigration applicants, screening of prison inmates and prostitutes. Four groups may be introduced exemplarily to show the effects or highlight the possible effects of mandatory testing and screening policies.

a. Mandatory Premarital Testing

Mandatory premarital testing programs for HIV-Antibodies in some states were introduced as a measure to reduce heterosexual and perinatal transmission of HIV infection. The rationale appears to be entirely socio-medical although it was government policy to introduce such programs. The authors of a study on such premarital screening concluded that the benefit of mandatory premarital HIV screening on HIV prevention is, in fact, unknown.[19]   They also hypothesized the cost of mandatory screening if all states of the U.S. were to adopt a policy to that effect. The testing of the about 2.4 million couples who apply annually for a marriage license in the U.S., at a cost of $35 per couple, would cost $167,230,000, which amounts to about 80% of the 211,889,000 Congressional appropriation to CDC for all public health control measures for the fiscal year 1988.[20] This would be a significant burden to public health and welfare budgets. The testing cost could be borne by the applicants but then one would also have to take into consideration that poor marriage applicants might in large numbers try to avoid the testing altogether by falsifying test result documents. That, in effect, would jeopardize the goals of the screening program altogether since the poor are likely to be at higher risk for HIV infection if one follows the statistics of HIV infection and AIDS among different population groups.

Mandatory premarital HIV-Antibody testing has turned out to be prohibitively expensive and entirely useless in the prevention of heterosexual and perinatal transmission of the AIDS virus. Illinois suspended its premarital testing program in September 1989, 20 months after its inception.

b. Testing of Job Applicants and Screening of Employees

Even before the CDC issued its guidelines for HIV-Antibody testing of health care workers, American businesses were eager to introduce their own testing programs for employees and new job applicants. Some of them could do so without problems. Several reasons are often cited for such testing. For businesses economic considerations are predominant. An employee or an applicant who tests positive may put too much of a financial burden on the company in case s/he develops AIDS while still in the service of that company. Insurance coverage as a part of the employee's benefits package may be hard to obtain or insurance companies may increase the premiums for the entire work force due to the fact that one or some of a company's employees are HIV-positive or have developed AIDS. Insurance companies fear that an increased number of HIV-positives or employees with AIDS will drain their financial resources. This may be particularly true due to the fact that HIV-positive people may try in large numbers to get into or remain in the job market in order to assure themselves at least of adequate medical care for a certain time should they become sick.[21]

Required testing of job applicants or periodic screening of the workforce, however, does not achieve anything with regard to the prevention of transmission of the AIDS virus. All those who are HIV-positive or have already developed AIDS can no longer be protected from the virus and neither testing nor screening are capable of preventing the transmission of the virus to the uninfected. Only consciousness raising, education, and appeals to behavioral change may be able to do that. Not allowing HIV-positive applicants to join the work force or relegating already employed HIV-positive employees gives employers undue powers to make decisions about an applicant's or an employee's fate which have nothing to do with an employee's current or future professional performance. Therefore, such testing and screening are unacceptable on ethical grounds.

It has already been reported, however, that a federal Court of Appeals in New Orleans affirmed a lower court ruling that a hospital may have the right to require an employee to be tested for HIV-Antibodies. The hospital argued that it had a right to know whether an employee would be the carrier of an infectious disease in order to comply with its own infection control policies, which required employees to report cases of infectious diseases to the infection control department.[22]

The *Philadelphia Inquirer* reported recently that the city's football team, the Eagles, had been tested for HIV-antibodies as a part of their routine physical examination in training camp.[23] The test results indicated that as of the testing date none of the players was carrying HIV. The reported result has to be taken, of course, with all due precautions and an understanding of the time a possible seroconversion may take. What is interesting about the Philadelphia Eagles case is the fact that the players claimed they did not know that they were tested. In fact, permission was obtained in standard consent forms before the physical exams as part of a general permission to perform blood tests in the course of the physical exams. A lawyer with the AIDS Law Project of Pennsylvania declared the tests illegally obtained, unjustified, and in clear violation of state employment laws and confidentiality laws.[24]

One can only speculate about the consequences, had any of the players tested HIV-positive. The fear among the athletes is already manifest. They expressed concern that anyone testing HIV-positive would be cut from the team. This concern was not shared by the team's president. He said that any HIV-positive testee "would have [been] referred to a physician for consultation or treatment."[25] This alone should not be reason enough to conduct a semi-secret HIV test on an entire team without adequate considerations for anonymity and confidentiality. If concerns about possible HIV infection among the players had arisen, the team could have embarked on an educationally enlightening course by bringing in experts to talk about possible virus transmission risks in "high risk" sports. The players could then have been encouraged to find out about their serostatus by visiting an anonymous and confidential testing center if they so desired. The way the issue was handled by the team's authorities only emphasizes the need for tight controls on an employer's ability to test or screen its employees at random for HIV. The players certainly expressed their powerlessness against the team authorities when they compared their situation to a "Catch-22."

c. Immigration Applicants

The United States Immigration and Naturalization Service has a program of mandatory testing of immigrants into the U.S. since 1987. At that time the U.S. Congress approved a Jesse Helms' amendment which added HIV infection to the list of excludable medical conditions. Foreigners who intend to apply for permanent residency status have to subject themselves to an HIV-Antibody test which has to be performed by an INS approved physician. The test results are entered on a chart bearing the name and other personal identification data of the applicant. The chart is sealed in an envelope and delivered to the INS with other immigration papers of the applicant, a measure which is intended to assure confidentiality of the test results.[26]

The INS also has the discretion to test temporary visitors if an immigration officer at the port of entry suspects for whatever reason that the entering visiting alien may pose a "public health risk" because of perceived HIV-infection. In 1989 the INS arrested and detained a Dutch visitor who was *en route* to an AIDS conference after the INS discovered AZT in his luggage. An immigration judge classified the visitor as an "excludable" alien but granted a waiver. The INS declared that the granting of the waiver should not be interpreted as precedent setting. Future HIV-infected temporary visitors may nevertheless be detained and held in administrative custody until the issue is legally settled.[27]

The organizers of the 1992 International AIDS Conference have decided not to hold the annual meeting in the United States (Boston) because of travel restrictions placed on HIV-Antibody-positve people implemented by the Bush administration. President Bush had a very cavalier response to the announcement of the conference organizers to choose a different site. In essence he said: "Oh, they'll find some place else to go." This is not exactly the kind of response one should expect from the leader of the country with the highest rate of HIV-infections and AIDS cases in the industrialized world.

With respect to testing of foreign visitors the World Health Organization also has advised against any kind of travel restrictions based on a person's serological status.[28] Making permanent residency and naturalization dependent on a negative HIV status of the applicant does in no way help to deal toward managing a health crisis. Travel barriers create undue human hardships by endangering the psychological well-being of human beings without providing a benefit to national or global public health.[29]

d. Screening of Male and Female Prostitutes

Many public health arguments have been made for the screening of prostitutes. They are members of a group at high risk for HIV-infection because of multiple sexual contacts, because of high-risk sexual practices, and because of possible parallel IV-drug use.[30] They also serve as a transmission link between the gay/bisexual community(ies) and the bisexual/heterosexual community(ies). Appeals for safer sex among prostitutes are not very fruitful because of client pressure for unrestricted sexual practices.

One of the major problems in screening prostitutes for public health reasons is the fact that prostitution is illegal in almost all localities of the United States, with the exception of the State of Nevada. Because of the illegal status of the profession, no accurate records about numbers and identities of prostitutes are available. Legalization, on the other hand, could be followed by licensing the exercise of the profession. Public health officials could get the necessary data to contact registered prostitutes periodically and call for HIV-Antibody tests with informed consent and pre- as well as post-test counseling in the course of periodic health check-ups and relicensing procedures.[31]

Legalization and licensing would also enable public health officials to educate prostitutes more effectively about safer sex practices. This would, in turn, empower the prostitutes to exercise more control with regard to their clients' requests for the performance of specific sexual practices that are deemed risky. Preconditions for legalization and licensing of prostitution are, of course, changes in social and political attitudes. As long as prostitutes of either sex are socially and politically discriminated against, as long as they are legally prosecuted in almost the entire United States, no public health measure which aims at the reduction or even elimination of HIV transmission *via* the prostitution route will be effective. A cursory look at the predominant moral sentiment in the United States may convince even the hopelessly optimistic person that the fulfillment of these preconditions is still a long way off.

Given the fact that prostitution is, in fact, illegal in the majority of locations in the United States, testing can only occur in the context of a law enforcement intervention toward job exercise prohibition on an individual basis. Prostitutes will try to avoid coming into contact with law enforcement agencies even more than they do already for fear that arrest may lead to imprisonment. Testing positive for HIV may lead to quarantine-like isolation. In such a case cooperation of prostitutes in any kind of testing program in the name of public health cannot be expected. Rather testing programs for prostitutes would reinforce the perception that governmental agencies, particularly law enforcement agencies, use HIV-Antibody testing purely for punitive reasons in the service of the execution of a judgmental moral verdict of society.

5. The Ethical Evaluation of Large Scale Testing and Screening Proposals.

From the four areas of HIV antibody testing and screening presented afore can be concluded that all types of testing and screening programs are of ambivalent ethical nature. Testing and screening as a result of government policies carries a punitive undercurrent. Actual medical rationales for the development of testing and screening programs are only rarely taken into consideration. Government policies are designed to achieve a political goal. They are judgmental in character in that they help establish a particular social norm to which human beings are expected to adhere.

In the case of HIV antibody testing the governmental goal is to say that a certain population group has been tested and that the momentary status of HIV-infection for that group is known. The observed time lag between infection with HIV and seroconversion, however, refutes this claim. No medical benefit can be expected from statistical knowledge alone.

The problem with public testing and screening policies is that the possibility exists for political abuse of the test results. Anonymity and confidentiality, even if assured by such policies, are relatively easy to circumvent, if so desired. Governmental institutions may at some point decide to exchange result files which may contain personally identifiable characteristics. Tracing of testees becomes relatively easy. The testees could become subject to social and political discrimination up to the point of exclusion from society through imprisonment, quarantine, or forced exile. The case of prostitute testing outlines such possibilities.

In the case of gay men, the loss of anonymity and confidentiality in the testing process could lead through enforced contact tracing to the identification of large gay population groups. They could be subjected to repeated antibody screening and, regardless of the test results, taken into "protective custody." Nazi policies toward homosexuals during the Third Reich should serve as a grim reminder. The authorities would cite three rationales for their punitive action. First quoted is the protection of the gay man from his own "dangerous" behavior, e.g., from engagement in sexual activity with partners.

The non-infected gay man has to be protected from infection by HIV-positive partners. For the HIV-positive gay man it means the prevention of infecting others with the virus.

The second rationale refers to the protection the authorities feel they have to provide to the endangered group "gay men" from carriers of the virus. The punitive measure of protective custody is exercised to benefit non-infected gay men by keeping them safe from any dangers. The authorities take over the entire realm of care for the human being and do no allow the affected person to make any decision about the conduct of his life by himself.

The third rationale is ethically the most unjustifiable. It is based on the authorities' moral choice to separate the orthodox majority society from its "deviant" challengers. HIV-Antibody screening is abused to state a particular political and moral point. It gives authorities the opportunity to act on their judgmental moral perceptions of orthodox and heretical social and sexual behavior. The government's power to test and screen degenerates into the opportunity to exercise socio-political control of undesirable social elements.

Testing and screening based on medico-scientific rationales may make sense if certain ethical rules are followed and limits respected.[32] Gaining statistical knowledge about the extent of HIV infection among the general population alone cannot be reason enough for large scale testing if it is not imbedded in an accessible and comprehensive counseling and caretaking system. This means that all testees have to receive pre- and post-test counseling. In case of positive test results, they have to be offered the opportunity for medical care as soon as the need arises.

Medico-scientific data collection in support of the development of restrictive social policies has to be rejected as incompatible with medical ethics. All testing and screening efforts have to be inspired by and directed toward healing or, where this is not or is no longer possible, toward the alleviation of pain and suffering. Mandatory testing and screening programs lack any justification on the grounds of therapeutic benefit. If name reporting and contact tracing are attached to mandatory testing policies, the result may, in fact, be counterproductive. It should also be refrained from introducing large scale voluntary testing and screening programs if protection against discrimination based on HIV status cannot be guaranteed unambiguously.

The testing game is a dangerous game in that it may be played with eyes closed with regard to an individual testee's human rights and privacy rights and with regard to the social well-being of significant population segments.

---

[1] See Christopher Joyce, "America's Hospitals Urged to Screen for HIV," *New Scientist* (August 4, 1990), p. 24.

[2] See Lewis and Montgomery, "The HIV-Testing Policies of US Hospitals," *JAMA* 264,21 (December 5, 1990), pp. 2764-2767, here: p. 2766.

[3] See Lewis and Montgomery, p. 2765.

[4] See Lewis and Montgomery, p. 2765.

[5] See *Morbidity and Mortality Weekly Report* (MMWR), 40, RR-8 (July 12, 1992).

[6] *Congressional Record—Senate* (July 11, 1991), S–9778; Amendment No. 734.

[7] *Congressional Record—Senate* (July 11, 1991), S–9779.

[8] See R. Weiss, "HIV can linger for years with no antibodies," *Science News* 135 (June 10, 1989), p. 340.

[9] *Michigan Recommendations on HIV-Infected Health Care Workers,* published by the Michigan Department of Public Health (October 28, 1991), p. 3.

[10] The Fedral guidelines were published under the title "Recommendations for Preventing Transmission of Human Imunodeficiency Virus and Hepatitus B virus to Patients During Exposure-Prone Invasive Procedures" in the U. S. Department for Health and Human Services *Morbidity and Mortality Weekly Report*, 40, RR-8 (July 12, 1991).

[11] The Michigan guidlines were published by the state's Department of Public Health and were made public on October 28, 1991.

[12] See *Recommendations*, p. 1.

[13] See *Ibid.*

[14] See *Recommendations*, p. 5.

[15] See *Ibid.*

[16] The CDC defines an invasive procedure in an appendix to the *Recommendations* as follows: "An invasive procedure is defined as 'surgical entry into tissues, cavities, or organs or repair of major traumatic injuries' associated with any of the following: '1) an operating or delivery room, emergency department, or outpatient setting, including both physicians' and dentists' offices; 2) cardiac catheterization and angiographic procedures; 3) a vaginal or caesarean delivery or other invasive obstetric procedure during which bleeding may occur; or 4) the manipulation, cutting or removal of any oral or perioral tissues, including tooth structure, during which bleeding occurs or the potential for bleeding exists'" (see *Recommendations*, p. 9).

[17] See "AMA, others oppose mandatory testing of doctors," *American Medical News* (March 11, 1991).

[18] See *Ibid.*

[19] Lyle R. Petersen, Carol R. White, and the Premarital Screening Study Group, "Premarital Screening for Antibodies to Human Immunodeficiency Virus Type 1 in the United States," *American Journal of Public Health* 80,9 (September 1990), pp. 1087-1090; here: p. 1090; Jack Mckillip, "The Effect of Mandatory Premarital HIV Testing on Marriage: The Case of Illinois," *American Journal of Public Health* 81, 5 (May 1991), pp. 650-653.

[20] See *Premarital Screening for Antibodies to Human Immunodeficiency Virus Type I in the United States*, p. 1090.

[21] See Alec Gray, "The AIDS Epidemic: A Prism Distorting Social and Legal Principles," *The AIDS Epidemic.* Ed. by Padraig O'Malley (Boston: Beacon Press, 1989), pp. 227-249.

[22] David Burda, "Appeals court upholds hospital's right to require emplyee AIDS testing," *Modern Healthcare* (September 3, 1990), p. 4.

[23] Mark Bowden, "Eagles were tested for AIDS, but they didn't know it," *The Philadelphia Enquirer* (November 1, 1991), D-1 and D-5.

[24] See *Ibid.*, D-1.

[25] See *Ibid.*

[26] See Masha Gessen, "HIV-Positive Foreign Nationals Face Discriminatory U. S. Exclusion Policy," *The Advocate* 583 (August 13, 1991), pp. 40-42.

[27] See Lawrence O. Gostin, "The AIDS Litigation Project: A National Review of Court and Human Rights Commission Decisions, Part I: The Social Impact of AIDS," *JAMA* 263,14 (April 11, 1990), pp. 1961-1970, here: pp. 1962-1963. The case referred to in the article is "*In re* Hans Paul Verhoef *v.* US Immigration and Naturalization Service,"(April 7, 1989).

[28] See *Ibid.*, p. 1963.

[29] See *Ibid.*

[30] See Alec Gray, "The AIDS Epidemic: A Prism Distorting Social and Legal Principles," *The Aids Epidemic.* Ed. by Padraig O'Malley, pp. 231-232.

[31] See Ronald Bayer, Carol Levine, and Susan M. Wolf, "HIV Antibody Screening: An Ethical Framework for Evaluating Proposed Programs," *The Aids Epidemic.* Ed. by Padraig O'Malley, pp. 173-187; here: pp. 180-181.

[32] See Carol Levine and Ronald Bayer, "The Ethics of Screening for Early Intervention in HIV Disease," *American Journal of Public Health* 79, 12 (December 1989), pp. 1661-1667; particularly: pp. 1663-1666.

VI. Mark R. Kowalewski:

Revisioning a Sexual/Social Ethic:
An Ongoing Journey

The majority of theologians and ethicists who have dealt with homosexuality in recent years have focused on the question of the legitimacy of sexual acts between members of the same sex in light of the Judeo-Christian tradition. These writings either reject the moral legitimacy of sex between men or between women, give qualified acceptance to such acts as morally inferior to sex between men and women, yet as an acceptable alternative for homosexual people, or, in a few cases, fully accept same sex acts in the context of loving relationships. These latter works have had an apologetic tone in which the author attempts to make a case for the legitimacy of homosexual acts through revisioning the tradition. Moreover, studies of homosexuality have generally been written most often by men who do not have a homosexual orientation, or at least do not embrace a gay identity. This is especially true of the first two types of responses.

The papers published in this volume, however, represent a new trend in writing about homosexuality and religion. These papers assume the legitimacy of gay sexual relationships. The writers have gone beyond apologetics and entered into a conversation concerning the quality of those relationships and what relationship gay sexuality has to other elements in gay men's lives. This holistic approach transcends the bounds of previous discourse fixated on the legitimacy or illegitimacy of sex acts. Moreover, these papers have emerged from the perspective of gay men writing about gay experiences in the context of their understanding of gay community. These writers speak from the position of those marginalized by the dominant discourse on sexuality as it has been expressed in the Judaeo-Christian tradition.

There are two central themes emergent in these papers. First, they present critiques of western hetero-patriarchal discourse regarding sexuality—a discourse which has had an impact on gay lives and the construction of gay lifestyles. Second, they attempt to reconstruct sexual ethics and integrate sexuality in the whole web of interpersonal and intergroup relations. The papers in this volume compose a thoughtful and scholarly contribution to a broader vision of gay-affirming ethics.

1. Dualistic Act-Centered Ethics: A Critique

From the perspective of the writers in this volume, traditionalist sexual ethics in the West have separated sexuality from the rest of life. Moral sexual expressions are understood in terms of actions which are right or wrong in themselves rather than evaluated within a context of a relationship between partners and in the context of the actor's life as a whole and with regard to his/her relationship to wider communities.

In his observations concerning Western constructions of male sexuality, Hopkins states that men fear losing control and individuality through sex. Separating sex from other aspects of one's life is a way of maintaining control and individual identity. He goes on to discuss the Western separation between "baser" and "higher" natures within human beings. This dualism splits the physical, emotional and sexual from the spiritual and rational—the body from the mind. In this perspective, the body and sexuality, divert men's attention from the higher and more noble call of the spirit and the intellect. Thus, people and things associated with sexuality are stumbling blocks which keep men from achieving their higher ends. Women, and by extension, homosexual men are perceived to be associated with the "baser self" and may be the objects of violence since they impede the progress of the "higher self".[1] Moreover, misogyny and homophobia are expressions of hatred not only of those who impede the realization of the "higher self," but really are an acting out of self-hatred, in that one hates one's sexuality. This dualism, sanctified in Western theological traditions, harms the individual since sexuality is not only separated from the rest of life, but is an object of shame and self-loathing. Sexuality is defined as an element of the self which leads one away from the spiritual path, rather than drawing one closer to the spiritual.

Kahn examines traditional Jewish sexual ethics. He notes that licit sexual expressions must occur within marriage, between two persons of the opposite sex through vaginal intercourse, with openness to procreation, with attention to the woman's pleasure and at specific times in the ritual calendar as well as specific times in the woman's menstrual cycle. Even the position in which the act is accomplished is legislated. Thus, only certain sex acts are legitimate at certain times and between certain people who are under certain obligations to eachother (i.e., marriage). These restrictions are based in notions of natural law in which the primary end of sexual expression is procreation. From the traditionalist perspective, this "law" governing sexual expression is grounded not in human understanding of sexuality at given historic epochs, nor in particular, historic and socio-economic relationships, but in the very nature of the universe as God commanded it and as encoded in the *Halachah*. Thus, any violation of these eternal laws is understood as a misuse of a divine gift and an inversion of the created order.

The traditionalist Halachic Jewish perspective is consistent with the natural law perspective of traditionalist Roman Catholic moral theology. In the Roman Catholic tradition, certain sexual acts are illicit regardless of the relationship between the actors because they defy the natural order as created by God. Thus, no genital sexual act between members of the same sex can ever be moral because the proper ends of sexual acts cannot be achieved by the actors. Sexual acts between persons of the same sex can never be fruitful or life-giving because they cannot be procreative.[2] The act is separated from the context of the relationship between partners.

Clark identifies a corollary of this act-centered sexuality in the experiences of gay men. Too often, he notes, sexuality is separated from the other aspects of gay men's lives. The pursuit of sexual pleasure is act-centered and anonymous. Nameless and faceless sexual liaisons make intimacy difficult and alienate gay men from relationships with others. Moreover, act-centered sexuality is related to the male fear of self-disclosure, of annihilation and loss of control. When men, including gay men, compartmentalize sexual acts they may feel more in control and do not feel they are losing their identity in intimate relationships with others. Clark goes on to argue that keeping "promiscuous distance" allows gay men to compartmentalize their sexual orientation and not fully integrate their gayness into the context of their lives as a whole.

2. *Revisioning a Sexual/Social Ethic*

In light of the critique of traditionalist Judeo-Christian sexual morality discussed above, the writers move on to revision sexual/social ethics in the context of their gay experience and in conversation with various religious traditions. They move beyond the dualistic and act-centered approach, as do many ethicists currently writing in religious studies or theology, to an ethic based in relationality and contextuality. The sexual, spiritual and social/communal elements of ethical discourse are not separated, but form a unity in which each element relates to the others.

Hopkins examines elements within Tibetan Buddhism which might be useful in revisioning Western ethics and spirituality. In Buddhist thought, Hopkins states, the experience of orgasm is not seen as an expression of the "baser self," but is a vehicle through which "grosser" levels of consciousness cease and through which more subtle forms of consciousness may become manifest. Indeed, orgasm may be a pathway to experiencing the "mind of clear light." Orgasmic experience can be a means to heightened spiritual consciousness. Sex is a vehicle for experiencing connectedness with the other, the one with whom one experiences sex, and with all other things. The Tibetan system attempts to overcome the fear of what is part of our basic nature—our sexuality. The body and mind/spirit form a unity where the body may be the vehicle of transcendence and spiritual experience.

A difficulty emerges in Hopkins' work in that he removes an element of thought from its ecological setting in a total system and world view. Hopkins sets the context for his discussion in the wider frame of Tibetan Buddhist thought. Yet, one must be cautious of such an endeavor without a fuller understanding of these concepts in the context of the religious, socio-economic, and political milieu out of which they emerge. For example, Hopkins notes that the type sexual yoga practice described by the Buddhist masters is a means of intimacy and relationality between the partners. However, he never gives evidence from the tradition concerning this point. The question here concerns the gender relations existing in the Tibetan Buddhist system when these spiritual texts were written. Is the spiritual seeker using the sexual partner as a vehicle for his spiritual experience? How much respect is given to the partner? Further, since women were excluded from the study of these practices, one cannot help but question the degree of relationality these tantric exercises were meant to evoke since they were exclusively heterosexual according to Hopkins' report. How useful is the Tibetan Buddhist experience to modern people in the West who do not share this tradition? While Hopkins does not give us answers to all these questions, he does give us an alternative perspective from an ancient tradition where the spiritual and sexual elements of the human person were seen as compatible. This alternative view is instructive for us in the West.

Kahn explores the tradition of Judaism and attempts to revision a relation centered ethic in response to traditionalist categories, but still within the context of the tradition. Like Hopkins, Kahn understands sexuality to be related to spirituality and the total experience of human beings. The morality of sexual expression, he notes, is not measured by permitted or forbidden acts, but by whether the relationship as a whole is just or unjust. Yet, sexuality forms a basis for the intimacy between lovers and that aspect of the relationship must be based on mutuality, equality and concern for the well being of the other. Moreover, the experience of an intimate relationship which is just in the private sphere strengthens lovers to open themselves to seek just relations in the public sphere and fuels the work for justice in society as a whole. Kahn echoes Carter Heyward in this view:

> Where there is no justice—between two people or among thousands— there is no love. And where there is no justice/no love, sexuality is perverted into violence and violation, the effects of which most surely

include rape, emotional and physical
battering, relationships manipulate by
control and competition and
contempt, and even war itself.[3]

Justice and passion should mutually inform our
intimate and broader social relations. Passion without
concern for the other results in violence and
oppression.

Clark argues that our sexuality should be a
vehicle for developing intimacy between persons in
relation:

> The erotic, or more concretely in our
> experience, our sexuality, becomes a
> meaningless, genitally-reduced notion
> *unless* we understand the erotic as
> part and parcel of our urges toward
> mutuality and human(e)ness.[4]

The erotic must be viewed as part of the whole web
of inter-relationship with others.

Pilant also discusses the need to go beyond the
self and explore relations between gay men and the
broader society. He asks what gay people can give to
heterosexual society. James Broughton also has
posed this question:

> Most gay activists are concerned with
> what society will do for them. They
> want acceptance, they want to be
> absorbed into the social fabric of the
> heterosexual mainstream... Look
> what heterosexual ethics has done to
> the earth with its shameless greed and
> its passion for war. We could show
> them how to love one another, we
> could teach them to trust
> comradeship, we could teach them the
> value of hilarity.[5]

Pilant also believes that the alternative discourse of the gay community can be beneficial to the broader society. The role gay people can play, he argues, is that of "wounded healers." The evil and persecution gay people have experienced needs to have redemptive value. Out of their own experience of woundedness, gay people can be the vehicle for healing in the broader society.

While the "wounded healer" metaphor may be a fruitful one for evoking the work of healing for ourselves and society, Pilant omits some crucial elements needed for establishing justice, noted by feminist writers, which have applicability to the quest of gay liberation. Beverly Harrison has noted:

> Where anger rises, there the energy to act is present... We must never lose touch with the fact that all serious human moral activity, especially action for social change, takes its bearings from the rising power of human anger.[6]

Pilant's metaphor embraces gay woundedness and gives an answer about gay people's gifts to the broader society, but does not take up the crucial place of our anger in the work of social justice for the gay community. He is all too quick to find redemptive meaning as a salve to ease our suffering. But the notion of redemptive suffering and sacrifice may easily result in a response of quiescence from the oppressed. I suggest that Pilant's view which asks us to have empathy with the suffering of oppressed others because we ourselves have been oppressed, needs to be coupled with an angry and passionate search for justice for ourselves and for others who experience oppression. Let our woundedness arouse our passion for justice. Furthermore, Pilant notes that gay liberation should not simply involve assimilation. While I agree with his view, we must work to realize the vision of liberation and social transformation. Pilant's view seems to pass over this crucial element in the work of justice.

Like several writers in this volume, Stemmeler seeks to move gay affirmative ethics beyond a narrowly defined focus on sexuality to a broader social view. His work deals with an issue of applied ethics, mandatory HIV-antibody testing. He asks when such testing is legitimate, if ever. When is testing abused to exploit those who are tested? This issue certainly has import for gay men who have been devastated by HIV disease. HIV testing, as Stemmeler notes, has been advocated by social conservatives, notably the "religious right," as a tool to stigmatize gay people. However, he goes beyond the gay community to note that testing has implications for other marginalized groups. It has implications for the poor who do not have enough resources and where HIV-positive serostatus may be the litmus test for exclusion from health care.

Stemmeler's work, differing in substance from the other papers in this volume, gives us an applied example of how the experience of stigma and oppression can move one beyond the self and one's own community. He shows us an example of making the connections with marginalized others and argues against the use of testing as a tool of power. He makes a plea for justice, fueled by anger, and brought forth from his experience as a gay man.

3. Conclusion

To use a phrase from Beverly Harrison's work, the writers in this volume have made the connections. They have noted that sexuality is not a separate and secret entity, and called us to integrate sexuality into our whole lives. They view sexuality as a vehicle for relationality between ourselves and the Other, as well as others with whom we are in relation—lovers, friends and families, the gay community, the broader society.

Moreover, these essays represent a variety of religious traditions and still the common threads noted throughout have emerged. These essays represent a small part of an ongoing conversation, a journey upon which the writers have embarked. The discourse within the gay community out of which this work emerges owes a tremendous debt to the work of feminists who have been continuing to engage in many of the issues discussed here for several years now. As gay men continue this conversation, we must be quick to hear the experiences of other communities, particularly those of lesbian feminists, and to discern our differences and our commonalities. The same must be said of discourse among gay men. What are our differences and our commonalities in light of our class, our ethnicity, our HIV status, or our religious tradition? In fact, a drawback of these essays is their failure to address the issue of difference among gay men. As we continue this journey, let me borrow from our elder brother Walt Whitman. "Camerado, I give you my hand... Will you come travel with me?" [7]

1 Beverly Harrison had discussed the connection between sexuality as an expression of the "baser self" and violence against women and gay men in "Misogyny and homophobia: the unexplored connections," *Making the Connections: Essays in feminist social ethics* (C. S. Robb ed., Boston, Beacon Press, 1985), pp. 135-151.

2 Until the 1960's official Roman Catholic moral theology defined procreation as the lefitimate end of sexual intercourse within marriage. In 1967, in *Humane Vitae,* Paul VI defined both procreation and the mutual fulfillment of the partners, as an expression of marital love, to be the dual ends of the conjugal act.

3 Carter Heyward, "Sexuality, Love and Justice," *Weaving the visions: New patterns in Feminist Spirituality* (J. Plaskow and C. P. Christ, eds.; San Francisco: Harper and Row, 1989), pp. 295-296.

4 J. Michael Clark with Bob McNair, "Masculine socialization and gay liberation: Excerpts," (in this volume), p. 11.

5 Mark Thompson, "In the service of ecstacy: An interview with James Broughton," *Gay spirit: myth and meaning* (M. Thompson ed.; New York: St. Martin's Press,) p. 205.

6 Beverly Harrison, "The power of anger in the work of love," *Weaving the Visions: New Patterns in Feminist Spirituality* (J. Plaskow and C.P. Christ, eds., San Francisco: Harper and Row, 1989) p. 220.

7 Walt Whitman, "Song of the open road," *Leaves of Grass* (New York: Modern Library, facsimile of the 1891-2 edition, no date supplied) p. 125.

VII. J. Michael Clark

Review of:
Families We Choose:
Lesbians, Gays, Kinship
by Kath Weston (New York: Columbia
University Press, 1991; hardcover $35).

A number of specifically gay male writers, most
notably those anthologized in Mark Thompson's *Gay
Spirit: Myth and Meaning* (St. Martin's, 1987), have
contended that gay or lesbian identity shapes a
uniquely "gay spirituality." Simultaneously, both
gay men and lesbians within the American Academy
of Religion have taken up the somewhat more
substantive endeavor of gay/lesbian theology, ethics,
and religious studies. None of these thinkers,
however, has as yet explored in detail the spiritual,
theological, or ethical value of constructed
gay/lesbian families. Now, a groundbreaking text
for such reflection has at last been published in
Columbia University Press' new lesbian and gay
studies series, "Between Men/Between Women."
Kath Weston's *Families We Choose: Lesbians,
Gays, Kinship* is an important first look, through the
fieldwork of an anthropologist, at how gay men and
lesbians construct their own families—based not nec-
essarily upon kinship, but based rather upon choice.
    Weston early raises the question as to whether
gay/lesbian families are "inherently assimilationist"
or a more "radical departure" from our customary
understandings (p. 2). Given gay theology's
realization of the extent to which gay people
generally and gay men in particular have been
bracketed by hetero-patriarchal society into a realm of
the "merely sexual" sequestered in the night, there

are good reasons for insisting that long term committed gay and lesbian couples and our surrogate family networks are in fact a radical challenge to such hetero-reductionism of gay and lesbian life. Weston herself acknowledges that the overly celebrated "nuclear family" is only an ideal in American society and does not realistically reflect the complicated meanings and implications of kinship for most people.

Moving from these introductory issues (ch. 1), Weston examines the tensions between gay/lesbian identity and families of origin, tensions which often compel us to create surrogate families of acceptance and unconditional love in lieu of our rejecting kinship families (ch. 2). In this context she also examines the dynamics of "coming out" (ch. 3) and provides a chapter of related case studies (ch. 4). In the second half of her text, Weston looks specifically at how gay/ lesbian families are constructed (ch. 5), the role of lovers in those chosen families (ch. 6), and the issue of parenting (ch. 7). She concludes by returning full circle to the politics of constructed families, in terms of both their political implications and their legal limitations in America—spousal insurance benefits, estate planning, etc. (ch. 8).

While Weston's text is clearly an important first resource—particularly given the historically developmental context in which she places each discussion—her work is not without its problems. For example, she initially appears so concerned to contradict the stereotype that gay men and lesbians are non-procreative loners that she risks making procreation a necessary qualification for gay/lesbian families. She over emphasizes that gay men and lesbians can still have biological children while overlooking the fact that a gay or lesbian couple and their circle of friends may equally well constitute a constructed family unit. The reader is finally relieved when she makes it clear that there is no monolithic definition for gay/lesbian families and that they may "incorporate friends, lovers, or children, in any combination" (p. 27, emphasis added). In fact, the families we construct do not require children and may be very fluid, including some kinship ties and excluding others, selectively including some gay/lesbian and some non-gay/les-bian friends, and even including our pets, gardens, and shared endeavors, broadening the concept of "constructed family" to include creating and valuing our gay and lesbian "homes." Weston is to be applauded, therefore, when she notes that gay/lesbian families challenge not procreation itself, "but the belief that procreation alone constitutes kinship" (p. 34), as well as when she concludes that our constructed families constitute "a more comprehensive attack on the privilege accorded to a biogenetically grounded mode of determining what relationships will count as kinship" (p. 35).

Just as her procreation discourse is initially misleading, so other problems with her discourse emerge later: The very phrase "families we choose," for example, sounds passive—as if such families existed a priori, merely awaiting our choosing. To speak instead of "constructed families" better reflects the real work of actively creating and sustaining a gay or lesbian familial network. Elsewhere, she confuses eroticism with sexuality. She insists that gay/lesbian friendships have developed since Stonewall to the extent that they are no longer erotically based. She uses the term "non-erotic" when what she really means is "non-sexual." Certainly post-AIDS many of our relationships are no longer based on sexual contact and activity. Nonetheless, we may still want to recognize with both feminist and gay liberation theology that we still experience ourselves as an "erotic community" or as a network of relationships erotically empowered toward common goals of justice-seeking and -making. Weston has failed to note the distinction that the erotic permeates all our relationships, but erotic community does not always imply sexual acting out.

Later, limiting her discussion of gay/lesbian spouses to an analysis vis-a-vis the Freudian mirror concept (the problem of narcissistic reflection) may have clinical value, but it offers little of pragmatic value for the average gay/lesbian reader. And, finally, while restricting her discussion of parenting to lesbian mothers appropriately reflects the author's existential subjectivity, she further limits her discussion to biological parenting. Not only does this bring her back to the initial confusion—again over emphasizing biology and procreation—but it also fails to provide any insights to gay/lesbian adoptive parenting. As thorough as her work has been to this point, an equally detailed analysis of the legal hurdles involved in, and the relational dynamics of, gay/ lesbian adoption would have added immeasurably to her book.

Apart from these weaknesses, Weston's strengths lie in her thoroughness—in describing the competing loyalties between kinship and chosen family obligations which holidays cause, or in describing the ways in which ethnic or native group experiences of oppression and resistant connectedness—as Black, as Latino/Latina—may take priority over gay/lesbian loyalty at times. Equally important is her valuation of the friendship paradigm—that constructed kinship is based on "an extension of friendship" (p. 118)—and her own further extension of this paradigm into an in-depth discussion of the development of gay/lesbian "community," from emphasizing our sameness in the 1970s to reasserting our diversity in the 1980s (pp. 122-136). Implicit in this discussion is the possibility that gay/lesbian families may ultimately be more liberating than gay/ lesbian community. Our constructed families can avoid the conformity demands of "the commu-nity" and community organizations, and can instead allow, encourage, and celebrate the very di-versity which so often causes conflict in community efforts.

Her greatest strength is the open-endedness of her political queries which refuse to see constructed gay/lesbian families as assimilationist capitulation. Our constructed gay/lesbian families can be, prophetically, better models of committed relationships (couples), homes, and families than the traditional, hetero-constructed, kinship-based marriages and families which exist in our patriarchal ethos. Based on an egalitarian friendship paradigm which adamantly rejects gender roles, our constructed families can become creative embodiments of the liberational impetus of our spirituality and our theological activity. Insofar as Weston's text serves as an important first resource for such liberational insight, her work becomes a valuable addition to the canon of gay/lesbian liberation.

Notes on Contributors

J. Michael Clark, Ph.D. (Emory University, 1980), is currently co-chair of the Gay Men's Issues in Religion Group of the American Academy of Religion and is both an "independent scholar" & a part-time instructor in the Freshman English Program of Georgia State University (Atlanta). Among his numerous publications are *A Place to Start: Toward an Unapologetic Gay Liberation Theology* (Dallas, TX: Monument Press, 1989); & *Theologizing Gay: Fragments of Liberation Activity* (Oak Cliff, TX: Minuteman Press, 1991). His spouse of four years is Bob McNeir who also contributed to this volume.

Jeffrey Hopkins, Ph.D. (University of Wisconsin, 1973), is Professor of Religious Studies at the University of Virginia where he has taught Indo-Tibetan Buddhist Studies and Tibetan language since 1973. He received a B.A. from Harvard University in 1963, trained for five years at the Tibetan Buddhist Learning Center in New Jersey, and received a Ph.D. in Buddhist Studies from the University of Wisconsin. He has published a dozen articles and twenty books on Tibetan Buddhism. At the University of Virginia he is Director of the Center for South Asian Studies and has founded programs in Buddhist Studies and Tibetan language. He is currently writing and analysis of Tibetan interpretations of the Mind Only doctrine of emptiness.

Yoel H. Kahn was ordained a Rabbi at Hebrew Union College–Jewish Institute of Religion, New York City, in 1985. Since then he served as a Rabbi at Congregation Sha'ar Zahav in San Francisco, a progressive reformed synagogue with a special outreach to Gays and Lesbians, their friends, families, and communities. He is pursuing doctoral studies at Graduate Theological Union in Berkeley, CA.

Mark R. Kowalewski, Ph.D. (University of Southern California, 1990), has published articles on Gay men and AIDS, as well as on religious responses to AIDS health crisis. After completion of his dissertation he worked as a post-doctoral research scholar with the Drug Abuse Research Group of the University of California, Los Angeles. For one year he taught religion and social sciences in the Theology Department of Xavier University, New Orleans, before returning in 1992 to his former position as researcher with the Drug Abuse Research Group at UCLA.

Bob McNeir survived being Gay in the military (Army). A native of Minnesota and Indiana, last stationed in Augusta, GA, he settled in Atlanta in the early 1980s and works for the combined Atlanta Newspapers in the payroll department. He and his spouse of four years, J. Michael Clark, raise vegetables and support a menagerie of dogs, birds, and fish. He helps keep Clark's theology and ethics connected to reality.

Craig W. Pilant, is a native of San Francisco, considers himself A Chicagoan, though he now lives in The Bronx. He received his B.A. from Loyola University, Chicago, and a M.A. in Medieval History from the University of Illinois at Chicago, which was followed by theological studies at Notre Dame. In addition to earning a M.A. in Education, he is now working on his dissertation in American Religious History at Fordham University, New York. His dissertation topic is on the American philosopher and theologian, Orestes Augustus Brownson, and the mainstreaming of American

Catholics in the mid-nineteenth century. At present, he is Director of Graduate Admissions for the Graduate School of Arts and Sciences at Fordham University, teaches undergraduates in Fordham College, and is Master of Queen's Court Residential College at Fordham.

Michael L. Stemmeler, Ph.D. (Temple University, 1990), is currently co-chair of the Gay Men's Issues in Religion Group of the American Academy of Religion and an assistant professor of religion at Central Michigan University. As leading co-editor of this series, he is the author of *Gays--A Threat to Society? Social Policy in Nazi Germany and the Aftermath*, in *Homophobia & the Judaeo-Christian Tradition* (series volume 1; Dallas, TX: Monument Press, 1990), pp. 69-93. He has co-produced a video on the experience of gay life and homophobia on the college campus, *In Our Own Words: Lesbian, Gay and Bisexual Students at CMU* (Mt. Pleasant, MI: CMU-A/V Productions, 1992). He is the author of several papers on medical ethics and AIDS, and is currently working in the areas of gay spiritual identity formation and the values of non-traditional relationships.